LETTING GOD BE GOD

TRADITIONS OF CHRISTIAN SPIRITUALITY SERIES

Traditions of Christian Spirituality Series

Letting God be God

The Reformed Tradition

David Cornick

SERIES EDITOR:
Philip Sheldrake

ORBIS BOOKS

Maryknoll, New York 10545

Founded in 1970, Orbis Books endeavors to publish works that enlighten the mind, nourish the spirit, and challenge the conscience. The publishing arm of the Maryknoll Fathers and Brothers, Orbis seeks to explore the global dimensions of the Christian faith and mission, to invite dialogue with diverse cultures and religious traditions, and to serve the cause of reconciliation and peace. The books published reflect the views of their authors and do not represent the official position of the Maryknoll Society. To learn more about Maryknoll and Orbis Books, please visit our website at www.maryknoll.org.

First published in Great Britain in 2008 by
Darton, Longman and Todd Ltd
1 Spencer Court
140-142 Wandsworth High Street
London SW18 4JJ

First published in the USA in 2008 by
Orbis Books
P.O. Box 308
Maryknoll, New York 10545-0308

FSC
Mixed Sources
Product group from well-managed
forests and other controlled sources

Cert no. SGS-COC-2953
www.fsc.org
© 1996 Forest Stewardship Council

Printed and bound in Great Britain.

Library of Congress Cataloging-in-Publication Data

Cornick, David.
  Letting God be God : the reformed tradition / David Cornick.
     p. cm. -- (Traditions of christian spirituality series)
  Includes bibliographical references.
  ISBN-13: 978-1-57075-779-2
  1. Reformed Church--Doctrines. I. Title.
  BX9422.3.C67 2008
  284'.2--dc22
                                    2007035815

CONTENTS

PREFACE TO THE SERIES

Nowadays, in the Western world, there is a widespread hunger for spirituality in all its forms. This is not confined to traditional religious people, let alone to regular churchgoers. The desire for resources to sustain the spiritual quest has led many people to seek wisdom in unfamiliar places. Some have turned to cultures other than their own. The fascination with Native American or Aboriginal Australian spiritualities is a case in point. Other people have been attracted by the religions of India and Tibet or the Jewish Kabbalah and Sufi mysticism. One problem is that, in comparison to other religions, Christianity is not always associated in people's minds with 'spirituality'. The exceptions are a few figures from the past who have achieved almost cult status such as Hildegard of Bingen or Meister Eckhart. This is a great pity, for Christianity East and West over two thousand years has given birth to an immense range of spiritual wisdom. Many traditions continue to be active today. Others that were forgotten are being rediscovered and reinterpreted.

It is a long time since an extended series of introductions to Christian spiritual traditions has been available in English. Given the present climate, it is an opportune moment for a new series which will help more people to be aware of the great spiritual riches available within the Christian traditions.

The overall purpose of the series is to make selected spiritual traditions available to a contemporary readership. The books seek to provide accurate and balanced historical and thematic treatments of their subjects. The authors are also conscious of the need to make connections with contemporary experience and values without being artificial or reducing a tradition to one dimension. The authors are well versed in reliable scholarship about the traditions they describe. However, their intention is that the books should be fresh in style and accessible to the general reader.

One problem that such a series inevitably faces is the word 'spirituality'. For example, it is increasingly used beyond religious circles and does not necessarily imply a faith tradition. Again, it could mean substantially different things for a Christian and a Buddhist. Within Christianity itself, the word in its modern sense is relatively recent. The reality that it stands for differs subtly in the different contexts of time and place. Historically, 'spirituality' covers a breadth of human experience and a wide range of values and practices.

No single definition of 'spirituality' has been imposed on the authors in this series. Yet, despite the breadth of the series there is a sense of a common core in the writers themselves and in the traditions they describe. All Christian spiritual traditions have their source in three things. First, while drawing on ordinary experience and even religious insights from elsewhere, Christian spiritualities are rooted in the Scriptures and particularly in the Gospels. Second, spiritual traditions are not derived from abstract theory but from attempts to live out gospel values in a positive yet critical way within specific historical and cultural contexts. Third, the experiences and insights of individuals and groups are not isolated but are related to the wider Christian tradition of beliefs, practices and community life. From a Christian perspective, spirituality is not just concerned with prayer or even with narrowly religious activities. It concerns the whole of human life, viewed in terms of a conscious relationship with God, in Jesus Christ, through the indwelling of the Holy Spirit and within a community of believers.

The series as a whole includes traditions that probably would not have appeared twenty years ago. The authors themselves have been encouraged to challenge, where appropriate, inaccurate assumptions about their particular tradition. While conscious of their own biases, authors have none the less sought to correct the imbalances of the past. Previous understandings of what is mainstream or 'orthodox' sometimes need to be questioned. People or practices that became marginal demand to be re-examined. Studies of spirituality in the past frequently underestimated or ignored the role of women. Sometimes the treatments of spiritual traditions were culturally one-sided because they were written from an uncritical Western European or North Atlantic perspective.

However, any series is necessarily selective. It cannot hope to do full justice to the extraordinary variety of Christian spiritual traditions. The principles of selection are inevitably open to question. I hope that an appropriate balance has been maintained between a sense of the likely readership on the one hand and the dangers of narrowness on the other. In the end, choices had to be made and the result is inevitably weighted in favour of traditions that have achieved 'classic' status or which seem to capture the contemporary imagination. Within these limits, I trust that the series will offer a reasonably balanced account of what the Christian spiritual tradition has to offer.

As editor of the series I would like to thank all the authors who agreed to contribute and for the stimulating conversations and correspondence that sometimes resulted. I am especially grateful for the high quality of their work which made my task so much easier. Editing such a series is a complex undertaking. I have worked closely throughout with the editorial team of Darton, Longman and Todd and Robert Ellsberg of Orbis Books. I am immensely grateful to them for their friendly support and judicious advice. Without them this series would never have come together.

PHILIP SHELDRAKE
University of Durham

PREFACE

The debts accumulated in writing a book like this are legion. The seed of the idea lay in a conversation with Philip Sheldrake when we were both on the staff of the Cambridge Theological Federation. Soon after I agreed to produce it, the United Reformed Church called me to be its General Secretary, which rather disrupted my writing pattern. My first debt of gratitude then, is to Philip, and to Brendan Walsh at Darton Longman and Todd, for their patience, perseverance and encouragement. Coupled with that is thanks to Brendan's colleagues at DLT for their professionalism and support.

My second debt is to the many scholars and writers who have informed my thinking about the Reformed tradition. A lifetime's reading around that subject means that some ideas will simply have been absorbed, so if I have unwittingly missed an attribution in the footnotes, my sincere apologies. Some of these scholars are not simply authors but friends, and I would like to record particular thanks to the Revd Professors David Thompson and Alan Sell, and Professor Clyde Binfield. For more than twenty years now their conversation, and their insight into and understanding of this tradition has enriched and challenged me.

My former students at Westminster College, Cambridge and my ministerial colleagues have suffered numerous experiments with this material in lectures and discussions at conferences. Thanks to them for questions and comments which led me to new conclusions.

My third debt is to the three communities which have sustained me during the writing of this book. The United

Reformed Church has nurtured my faith for most of my life, and in its struggles and joys I have learnt something of what it means to be a disciple of Jesus. There is no greater gift than that. For the last fifteen years that has been mediated to me particularly by the ministers and members of Emmanuel United Reformed Church in Cambridge, a wonderful spiritual 'home'. A very different kind of community, Robinson College, has been my academic home for the last nine years. A more congenial atmosphere in which to think and write is hard to imagine.

My fourth debt is to my Deputy, Ray Adams, whose friendship and laughter lightens the working day, and whose enormous capacity for hard work has allowed me the freedom to finish this book.

Finally, and by no means least, thanks to my family; to Peter who read and corrected the entire manuscript at a critical stage, to Peter and Andrew who have learnt to cope with an absent father (in more ways than one), but above all to Mary whose love and tolerance has even extended to coping with the untidy piles of books and cascades of paper escaping from the study that seem to go with the business of writing.

DAVID CORNICK
Advent 2007

INTRODUCTION: THE REFORMED TRADITION AND THE STUDY OF SPIRITUALITY

Books on 'Reformed spirituality' are as rare as hens' teeth. The words themselves seem in uneasy partnership. The meanings of both words seem clear until definitions are attempted. Then it quickly becomes apparent that both words have hidden pitfalls. They are dangerous words in theological discourse, let alone at twilight. Beyond the mire of ambiguity, they are mutually suspicious words, for both find their natural home in the rhetoric of theological and ecclesiastical division.

'Reformed' is a label which is commonly used to distinguish the rigorous emphasis of the Swiss Reformers on reformation, according to scriptural principles, from 'Lutheran' and 'Catholic' perceptions of the Church. However, there is also a sense in which all Protestant churches are by nature 'Reformed', and during the sixteenth century 'Reformed', 'Protestant' and 'evangelical' were used almost synonymously.[1] The word can therefore be a theological umbrella which lends shelter to such diverse souls as Dutch Anabaptists and certain Elizabethan bishops. Some Anglican thinkers like J. I. Packer would still consider themselves true representatives of the Reformed tradition, the rightful heirs of the English Puritans. A more telling problem in the quest for definition is the convergence of Congregational and Presbyterian churches in several united churches across the world and in the World Alliance of Reformed Churches, formed in 1970 from the union of the International Congregational Council and the

World Alliance of Presbyterian Churches. Their spiritual ancestors would have been astonished, for in the sixteenth century Catholics and disciples of the magisterial Reformers were equally terrified of the sectarians of the radical Reformation, and persecuted them grievously. Hidden within the contemporary use of the word, then, is an historical conundrum. Ecumenism's joy has been the marriage of such Montagues and Capulets. However, it is not surprising that a sensitive ear sometimes hears distant rumblings of far-off battles, even if both families revered Calvin as a prince amongst theologians. Definition and delineation will both be needed before we can discuss 'Reformed' spirituality.

'Spirituality' is an even more perplexing word. In common usage it is often (wrongly) taken to mean the opposite of 'material' – the psychic or the supernatural. Such a dualistic understanding is of little help in the era of the human genome. The physical and the non-physical cannot be so easily sundered. 'Spirituality' derives from the Latin *spiritualitas*, itself a translation of the Greek *pneuma* and *pneumatikos*. In Paul's thought the life of the spirit is not opposed to the life of the body (*soma*) but to that of the flesh (*sarx*). *Sarx* is a powerful and resonant word in Paul's thought. It means not simply physical flesh (as in, e.g., 2 Cor. 12:7, the thorn in the flesh) but a whole 'earthy' way of life (e.g. 1 Cor. 15:39; 2 Cor. 4:11), an entire ecology of living apart from God (2 Cor. 10:1–5). *Sarx* is not a dualistic concept for Paul, for it embraces thought and feeling and emotion as well as the obviously physical. Life in the Spirit is therefore equally holistic, equally conscious of the integration of the human person. Paul is not a dualist. He understands the spiritual life as that of a person in whom the Spirit of God is 'dwelling', and his measure of the two ways of life is essentially ethical and moral (Gal. 5:22ff).

That sense can still be found in the writings of Aquinas, but by the time he wrote the influence of scholasticism had brought about a different understanding that opposed the 'spiritual' with the 'material'. That sense too can be found in

Thomas. Between the thirteenth and sixteenth centuries the word was mainly used in yet another, juridical, sense, for 'spirituality' became synonymous with 'the clerical estate'. It re-emerges into the world of devotion and relationship with God in the seventeenth century, firstly in France, and then in England. It was used supportively of a personal relationship with God, but also critically of excess, whether Quietist or Enthusiastic. Indeed, during the eighteenth and nineteenth centuries it was used more outside mainstream Christianity than within it, and not until the early years of the twentieth century did it re-establish itself in theological discourse, at first in French Catholic writings and then in English translations of them.

If the word is slippery, the practice once was not. Indeed, theology and spirituality were synonymous until the relocation of theology into the academy during the High Middle Ages. Theology's courtly love affair with philosophy heralded the beginnings of its long journey towards modernity and 'rational' methodology. 'Mystical theology', the gleaning of wisdom from prayerful reflection on the Scriptures, became in consequence an almost exclusively monastic preoccupation. However, as theology both created and critiqued the Enlightenment, piety became at best a non-academic pursuit, and mysticism deeply suspect. Post-Enlightenment uses of the word 'spirituality' therefore fragmented in at least three ways. First, it was used by those who wanted to speak of a 'mystical' dimension to the spiritual life. Secondly, it was used to distinguish the study of the spiritual life from the systematic study of dogma, particularly in the Roman Catholic Church. And thirdly, it began to be used increasingly in discourse about the nature and value of religious experience.[2] In contemporary use spirituality is, of course, not an exclusively Christian word. It is a word much in vogue, largely thanks to the breakdown of the modernist consensus and the emergence of the so-called New Age movement. If what is meant by 'spirituality' is that which animates and inspires at the deepest level of being human, then there are many spiritualities, including Buddhist, Hindu, Marxist and secular varieties.

In the Christian traditions, however, the severance of spirituality from theology pushed the guidance of Christian lives to the margins. There, initially in Roman Catholic seminaries, but then ecumenically as clerical education gradually professionalised, in textbooks of 'spiritual theology' or 'practical theology', spirituality began to demand attention. 'Spiritual theology' gained an official foothold within the Catholic theological curriculum in 1919, and was included in the Vatican's *Deus Scientiarum Dominus* (1931). Its shape was essentially Thomist, subordinate to dogmatic theology which taught the faithful what to believe, and to moral theology which taught them how to avoid sin. 'Spiritual theology' in its turn was subdivided into 'ascetical' and 'mystical' theology. As Sandra Schneiders notes, 'it was deductive in method, prescriptive in character, and concerned primarily with the practice of personal prayer and asceticism.' These were confessor's handbooks. Their Protestant equivalents were handbooks of pastoral practice.[3]

The danger for the Christian theologian after Einstein is that 'spirituality' might be cast adrift from its ethical and political moorings into a sphere of pure interiority. Techniques of prayer and the cartography of human relationships with God are important, but they are inadequate and imprecise if they are severed from the living of the Christian life. Our lives are 'hid with Christ in God', not just as choral evensong sweeps over us or a profound sermon moves us to new depths, but as we sit waiting in the doctor's surgery, agonise over impossible dilemmas, and do the shopping in our local supermarkets. That is one reason why the Orthodox theologian Alexander Schmemann has suggested that we should talk about 'Christian living' rather than 'spirituality'.[4] 'Spirituality', then, has to do not simply with experience, but with cultural context, for no experience is unmediated. It is also to do with faith as it is experienced and lived out, and therefore with ethical and political life, because that is the theatre of human activity.

Sheldrake observes an ecumenical convergence around this principle. 'Spirituality' inclines to eclecticism rather than sectarianism, and is thus a better expression of catholicity than the spiritual theologies which dominated Roman Catholic writing prior to Vatican II.[5] Spirituality as it has emerged over the last quarter of a century in Western Christianity is, he suggests, inclusive rather than exclusive, theologically responsible, more concerned with the mystery of life before God than prescribing paths to travel, and ethically and morally committed. This new understanding of the study of Christian spirituality is an altogether more holistic, if necessarily more ragged, discipline. It is concerned with 'the conjunction of theology, prayer and practical Christianity.'[6] That is to say, its subject matter is the relationship between God, the human person, the Christian community and the world.

Students of spirituality are therefore eager conversation partners with moral theologians, who are now themselves concerned with virtue and character as much as actions; with historians, who themselves are increasingly fascinated by the relationship between belief, expression and culture, or what some call *mentalités*; with psychologists and empirical scientists, who are themselves concerned with how human beings construct and construe wholeness. As Rowan Williams noted, spirituality is

> far more than a science of interpreting exceptional private experiences; it must now touch every area of human experience, the public and the social, the painful, negative, even pathological byways of the mind, the moral and relational world ... an acceptance of this complicated and muddled bundle of experiences as a possible theatre for God's creative work.[7]

The development of spirituality as a theological subdiscipline cannot be divorced from the broader history of the Christian churches. The twentieth century is sometimes

called 'the ecumenical century'. The new air of trust and
understanding prompted by the Edinburgh Missionary Conference of 1910 and its continuation committees created a
new atmosphere and encouraged the brave to look over the
barricades, and the radical to knock a few breaches in
them. Spirituality and ecumenism have been in creative
interaction as Christians have discovered anew what unites
them, and in the light of that reviewed the causes of division. That in turn has encouraged Christians to share
the riches of their traditions with each other, and to be surprised and delighted that forms of devotion and prayer
which seemed alien are rich with blessing. It is striking
that two of the most influential religious communities of the
century, Iona (1930s) and Taizé (1940s), were founded by
Reformed ministers, George MacLeod of the Church of Scotland and Roger Schutz of the Swiss Reformed Church respectively. They are prophetic figures, to whom we will return.

The practical consequences of ecumenism and new landscapes of worship and prayer have been more readily absorbed amongst the Reformed than changes within the
theological sub-discipline of spirituality. There are two reasons for that. First, 'spiritual theology' did not have a natural
home within the Reformed theological curriculum. It, and its
renewal in the early years of the twentieth century, were
regarded as areas of specific Catholic interest. Unlike dogmatics or ethics, the Reformed could claim no traditional
expertise in this branch of theological science. Only recently
have Reformed writers begun to explore the texture of their
spiritual practice in a way that is compatible with the new
contours of the academic study of spirituality, as Howard
Rice has done in his groundbreaking *Reformed Spirituality –
An Introduction for Believers*.[8] Second, for good theological
reasons the Reformed are inherently suspicious of human
experience as a proper starting place for the theological
enterprise. As a wise minister once said to a young colleague,
'Stop worrying about the state of your soul, and get on with
the job God's given you to do.' Reformed theology has long

played Martha to Catholicism's Mary, for if classical Thomist theology is about ultimately attaining the vision of God, the goal of Reformed theology is participation in God's divine activity.

Such stereotypes are a guide to truth, but rigid adherence to them risks impoverishment. It has been a joy to see the growth of retreat movements and silence within Reformed churches, to watch the alacrity with which ministers and lay people alike sign up for Ignatian retreats and days of Benedictine prayer. The trouble is, the Reformed have convinced themselves that spirituality is something other Christians do, and they are therefore unaware of the depth of their own tradition and unable to share it. Perhaps a redefinition of spirituality, such as Sheldrake's 'the conjunction of theology, prayer and practical Christianity', might help the Reformed recover God's astonishing generosity to them across four centuries. No tradition that includes such towering physicians of the soul as Richard Baxter, Jonathan Edwards, Isaac Watts, John Baillie, Olive Wyon, George MacLeod and Roger Schutz is either uninterested in spirituality or spiritually impoverished.

Our spiritualities are the product of a complex interacting web of influences. At the heart of all of them lies, of course, the work of the Holy Spirit, but the form of that influence is mediated through personality, ecclesial tradition, national and regional culture, and experience. The Reformed theologian John Oman wrote:

> God does not conduct his rivers, like arrows, to the sea. The ruler and compass are only for finite mortals who labour, by taking thought, to overcome their limitations, and are not for the Infinite mind. The expedition demanded by man's small power and short day produces the canal, but nature, with a beneficent and picturesque circumambulancy, the work of a more spacious and less precipitate mind, produces the river. Why should we assume that, in all the rest of His

ways, He rejoices in the river, but in religion, can use no adequate method save the canal?[9]

The modern study of spirituality is concerned with tracing that river's meandering path, or, to change the metaphor, with exploring the ways in which a particular *habitus* is formed. So, an exploration of the distinctiveness of Reformed spirituality will be concerned with mapping the subtle ways in which specifically Reformed understandings of the ways of God are mediated. What makes this river different from Catholic, Methodist and Anglican rivers? Is there, indeed, any difference in this ecumenical age?

Rowan Williams argues that difference and distinctiveness lie behind both the emergence of the Church in the early Christian centuries and the re-configuration of the shape of the Church that marked the Reformations of the sixteenth century.[10] Early Christians, he observes, defined themselves in three ways which would have been strange to their contemporaries, both Jewish and Graeco-Roman. First, they called themselves *hagioi*, people who were holy or sacred. Second, they met together in *ekklesiai*, civic assemblies. Third, they described themselves as *paroikoi* or *paroukontes*, resident aliens. Here were a group of people who were claiming that their citizenship belonged elsewhere, and that they were therefore outsiders from the imperial structures. They deliberately distanced themselves from civil structures, refusing to serve in the army or to hold civic office. That, he suggests, is why the narrative of martyrdom becomes the distinctive form of Christian writing in the century after the New Testament. Martyr narratives begin, 'The *ekklesia* of God living as resident aliens in X, to the *ekklesia* of God living as resident aliens in Y.' This separate, distinctive identity is essential, and the literature of martyrdom is its legitimation. This concern for difference and distinctiveness lies behind the passionate concern of the second- and third-century Church with purity and discipline. Rigorism is a fear of the loss of sacredness. The body is where divine power resides.

Augustine's response to the Donatists critically redefined that understanding. His argument that a bishop's sacramental actions were not invalidated by his apostasy relocated the holiness of the Church in the Christ-bringing Spirit, who 'comes into us through a radical putting aside of self-reliance'. The integrity of the Church is to be located, therefore, not so much in visual continuity as in faithfulness to the activity of God within it.

Pre- or post-Augustine, however, the early Church is about difference, a difference defined by what God does in Christ, a difference born witness to by resident aliens and marked by martyrdom. The Reformation, Williams goes on to suggest, is at heart about the Reformers' perception that the Church had forgotten that it exists solely by 'the direct will and agency of God'. What Luther does, he says, is place the gratuity of God's action at the centre of the agenda. God's justice is not about judgement, but about his free act which makes us just through no merit of our own. This has two crucial effects. First, it frees believers from an obsession with making themselves acceptable to God. Second, if believers themselves are the focus of God's activity, it is reasonable to expect that activity to flow into ethics, politics and service of the world. Whilst Calvinism and Lutheranism developed different understandings of the relationship between church and state, both are in essence about worldly spirituality in the sense that the division between 'sacred' and 'secular' has been broken down.[11]

So, according to Williams, Christian living, and therefore spirituality, is about 'difference'. Drawing on Michel de Certeau's work on Catholic spirituality in the sixteenth and seventeenth centuries, he is struck by the similarities between the Protestant and Catholic worlds. The instability and incompleteness of the self in Carmelite writings, and Luther's quest to root the self in the alien love of God, have shared characteristics, not least a deep suspicion of religious experience and a profound sense of homelessness in this world. Take the love of God away, as de Certeau pointed out, and you are left essentially with the 'desiring, dissatisfied' modern self.

Williams's argument is fecund and suggestive. His clear mapping of the history of 'difference' as the defining characteristic of the early Church and the Reformation is particularly helpful. However, he has little to say about the Calvinist and Reformed traditions. In the chapters that follow, that concept of 'difference' will be used as a tool to interrogate the Reformed tradition, to discover if there is a distinctive Reformed spirituality.

If 'denominational' difference provides the vertical grid for study of the Reformed matrix, ethnic and national contexts provide the horizontal. George MacLeod once wrote in a letter to Duncan Finlayson:

> You and I come of Calvinistic stock: and Calvinism was probably a justified protest against the raging romantic subjectivism of the Celtic character, with its warlocks, witches and whimsy. Now that warlocks belong to lore, and witches to psychopathology, and whimsy died with J. M. Barrie, Calvinism is now a concept of the mind, but its virus still lurks in the marrow of our psyche ...

MacLeod, one part Celtic mystic, one part evangelical, had deep respect for his roots in Scottish Calvinism, but was acutely aware of its limitations.[12] The 'difference', the virus, was in his marrow. That is not a bad definition of the particularity of a spiritual tradition.

This book is about the taxonomy of that virus. It will attempt to be sensitive to both Reformed 'difference' and context, and it will reveal a richer, subtler and more nuanced tradition than is generally appreciated. It is about 'Reformed' spirituality, not Anabaptist, Celtic, national or ecumenical spiritualities, although Reformed spirituality is often found in conjunction with one or more of them. All of those are rich traditions in their own right, worthy of separate studies. With that proviso, Chapter 1 sets out the history of the Reformed tradition. Chapter 2 explores the ways in which worship and private prayer have moulded Reformed people. Chapter 3 begins with an exercise in spiritual archaeology, for historically the Reformed tradition gave undue prominence to the doctrine of predestination. The shortcomings of that emphasis are then balanced against the strengths of a spirituality of election. Chapter 4 ventures into the worlds of art and space, and the ways in which the Reformed utilised both in the expression of a 'worldly' spirituality. The final chapter probes the Reformed understanding of church, community and ecumenism through the work of those two prophetic Reformed figures of the twentieth century, George MacLeod and Roger Schutz.

1 WHO ARE THE REFORMED?

The Reformations of the sixteenth century and the Reformed

The emergence of the Reformed as a distinct Christian community is inextricably intertwined with the Reformations of the sixteenth century. In 1500 there was one Church in the West. By 1550 there were many. The reasons are complex and fiercely disputed by historians. Scholarly study of the Reformations of the sixteenth century over the past 20 years shows that, far from being corrupt and irrelevant to the lives of ordinary people, the rituals and practice of the late medieval Church were effective, helpful and cherished. The Church was far from ripe for reform. Luther was simply the last in a long list of theologians and activists who argued passionately for change in the Church. He said little that had not been said before. What emerges from contemporary study of the Reformations of the sixteenth century is a more complex, multi-faceted process of change and revolution.

It is in those turbulent, complex processes which dominated the small towns and cities of Germany and Switzerland in the 1510s and 1520s that we find the origins of the Reformed tradition. It could be argued that the immediate cause of Luther's protest in Wittenberg in 1517 was a pastoral crisis.[1] Martin Luther was not just a professor of theology. He was also a priest who was passionately concerned about those in his pastoral care. It was what he learned in the confessional about the activities of the indulgence-seller Johannes Tetzel, just over the border of Saxony in Brandenburg, that led to the posting of the 95 theses against indulgences. An indulgence was a way of saving yourself, or one dear to you who had died, from the purifying pains of purgatory. If you were truly contrite, confessed to a priest, and then purchased an indulgence, the Church had the power to remit some or all of that temporal punishment. Johannes Tetzel, a fine Dominican preacher, was doing excellent business, and Luther was incensed. That sense of anger only intensified when he later discovered that his young archbishop, Albrecht of Mainz, had sanctioned the indulgence to raise funds to repay a loan from the Fugger banking house which he had taken out to pay the fee demanded by Rome to allow him to hold the sees of Magdeburg and Halberstadt in plurality with Mainz.

The mere thought that salvation could be bought was anathema to Luther, for his academic studies were in the theology of St Paul, and particularly justification by faith. That was confirmed by his own agonised spiritual journey. No one could have striven harder to be a good monk and please God by good works than Luther. But obsessive strictness and abundant charity did not work, and it was only as he read Paul that he discovered that salvation comes by surrender to God in Christ. It is God's work in Christ that saves humanity, and that salvation is appropriated through the simple act of faith. Luther's spiritual journey and his academic studies came together as he protested vigorously about Tetzel, publishing his 95 theses, which was the normal way to activate an academic debate.

There it might have remained, but for the new invention of the printing press. Pamphlet warfare erupted. Luther's views began to spread like wildfire, and in 1520, after a series of legal and theological disputations, Luther was excommunicated.

After this, Elector Frederick of Saxony wisely took him out of circulation for a while, protecting him in the Wartburg Castle. As Gordon Rupp said, it paid dividends, for 'some of [Luther's] finest writings, and the immense German Bible derived from his Patmos.'[2] A power vacuum was left in

Wittenberg, though, into which stepped (amongst others) the Most Reverend Lord Professor Andreas Bodenstein von Karlstadt, Doctor of Theology, Doctor of Canon and Secular Law, Archdeacon and Canon of All Saints Wittenberg, Dean of the Faculty of Theology. Ambitious and angular, litigious to a fault as an archdeacon, able yet neither scintillating nor ground-breaking as a theologian, he was nonetheless a brave man who stood beside his colleague Martin Luther in the turbulent years between 1518 and 1521, when the whole world seemed against them. As the reforming temperature increased in Wittenberg in the autumn of 1521, Karlstadt wrote tracts and encouraged academic disputations on clerical marriage, vows and communion in both kinds. Then, defying the civil authorities, on Christmas Day 1521 he celebrated a simple communion service with no sacrificial language and no vestments, offering the people both bread and wine. The following day he announced his engagement to Anna von Mochau, the none-too-pretty daughter of a poor gentleman, and a fortnight later secured his place in history by becoming the first Reformer to marry.[3]

The innately conservative Luther rapidly distanced himself from his former colleague, although their friendship was never quite destroyed. However, Karlstadt was a radical not from choice, but conviction. At the heart of his spirituality was Scripture. It was there that he sought guidance, and there he found what he believed to be a simple, complete denunciation of images in the ten commandments:

> You shall not make for yourself an idol, whether in the form of anything that is in the heaven above, or that is on the earth beneath, or that which is in the water under the earth. You shall not bow down to them or worship them: for I the Lord your God am a jealous God ...
>
> (Exod. 20:2)

'I say to you,' Karlstadt commented in his *On the Abolition of Images* (1522), 'that God has forbidden images with no less diligence than killing, stealing, adultery and the like.'[4]

Prohibited by Scripture, dangerous, maybe even devilish, statues, paintings, stained glass and other forms of religious art have to go. Art is so cherished in our society that we automatically assume that anyone who issues such an edict is an uncultured ruffian. Karlstadt wasn't. He was cultured, highly educated, a capable scholar. It was not that he and later Reformers did not value art. They did, profoundly, and they were happy and content to promote both civic and domestic art. Their objection to the use of art in church was entirely theological. God was so great, so mysterious and wonderful, so beyond the reach of mind and the capacity of the human imagination, that he could not even be hinted at by the greatest of artistic achievements. Karlstadt wrote: 'all the pictures on earth put together cannot give you one tiny sigh towards God.' Finite things cannot contain the infinite. Only God's love and grace can bridge the unbridgeable gap between God and humanity. God did that in Christ, as Scripture and the Lord's Supper bear witness. As Karlstadt put it, 'The Word of God is spiritual, and it alone is useful to the believer.'[5]

This theology emphasised the otherness of God, God's transcendence. In the early decades of the sixteenth century that was shocking, for the close immanence of God had defined religious culture for a thousand years. The world was alive with the presence of God, crackling with the electricity of holiness, in the sacraments of the Church, the physicality of the saints and their relics weaving a web between heaven and earth, in holy places and holy things, and most supremely in the eucharistic host – God made manifest daily in the lives of the people of God.

The critique of that world was launched with biting satirical incisiveness by Erasmus of Rotterdam, humanist, professor of Greek, editor of the Greek New Testament, and in the end, devoted follower of the old ways. In *Enchiridion* (1503) Erasmus made it clear that the visible world could not contain the invisible and that true religion belongs to the invisible realm. Karlstadt was deeply influenced by Erasmus but he fused Erasmus's dualism with his own relentless scriptural logic. It was a potent brew. The recipe was to be slightly varied by the Swiss Reformers, but none of them diluted its destructive potential. Here was the power to lay waste the vibrant, tactile world of medieval immanence. Luther studiously avoided it, developing a theology which allowed the material and the divine to touch and intermingle. The Swiss Reformers amongst whom Karlstadt was to make his home, made his theological hallmark their own.

His was only one influence amongst many, though. Zwingli was a noted humanist, educated at Vienna and Basel. He too was a passionate admirer of Erasmus, drinking in the master's transcendentalism.[6] The pseudonymous *On the Old God and the New* (1521), written the year before Karlstadt's *On the Abolition of Images*, both defined idolatry as 'a raising of the creature over God through the deception of the devil' (a definition which would become standard in Reformed circles) and proposed that God is honoured only when his commands are obeyed, not by the work of human hands.[7]

Zwingli's own theology was deeply scriptural. From the time he was appointed as people's priest at the Great Minster in Zurich in 1519, he used the method of *lectio continua* to guide his preaching ministry, and his reforming programme proceeded according to the principle of testing the biblical foundations of all practices in the life of the Church to see if they promoted the central message of Scripture, namely the redemption of the world in Jesus Christ. Biblical authority was central. Behaviour had to accord with the commands of Scripture. Anything that obstructed Scripture was disobedience.[8] That was as true of the liturgical life as the moral. True religion, said Zwingli in his *Commentary on True and False Religion* (1525), was 'that which clings to the one and only God ... Nothing, therefore, of ours is to be added to the Word of God, and nothing taken from his Word by rashness of ours.'[9] It was inevitable that such a theological method would quickly raise questions about a range of practices – from the veneration of the saints and tithing to the use of music and the works of art in church.

From 1523 onwards Zwingli's preaching encompassed opposition to images, and isolated outbreaks of iconoclasm began to mark the city's life. Tension rose until the council decided to deal with the matter with a public disputation, the Second Zurich Disputation of October 1523, which ended by condemning the Mass and images. However, it was not until the following June that the council eventually called for the orderly removal of images from the city's churches. In two weeks, gone were the 'statues, paintings, murals, altar decorations, votive lamps and carved choir stalls' which had shaped Zurich's spiritual perceptions for centuries.[10] In their place came white-washed walls, the centrality of the Word, and a plain table for the observance of the Lord's Supper. Here was no distraction, simply the austerity that turned the mind to the words that opened the door into the invisible world where the holy and transcendent God dwelt.

Reformed spirituality begins its journey there, surrounded by white walls, concentrating on Scripture read and proclaimed, for the Spirit works through the words of the Bible and those who expound it to feed the faithful and bring them into the nearer presence of God. It is a whole new order, a revolution built on God's Word, a rediscovery of the aniconic spirituality powerfully witnessed to in the Jewish Scriptures and echoed in the iconoclast controversy of the eighth century.

These embryonic Reformed theologians had accidentally discovered simplicity. This was to have far-reaching consequences in the Reformed tradition. It was to be expressed theologically and politically in the perspicuity of Scripture. Scripture was expected to cohere and make sense, and to speak to the honest believer. Revered though teachers and preachers were to become, there was never any doubt that the Scriptures belonged to the people of God, not to a professional caste. It informed the nature of Reformed worship. What mattered above all was Scripture. It needed to be heard and understood, and the liturgy was to be used to enable that, not distract from it. It also determined the nature of

Reformed aesthetics, where economy and elegance are instinctive.

If the first manifestation of Reformed spirituality was iconoclasm, its midwife was humanism. There was a close,
symbiotic relationship between the Reformed tradition in its
earliest days and the humanist project. Humanism in the
sixteenth century was about the recovery of the power and
wonder of the ancient civilisations of Greece and Rome. That
recovery took place primarily through words, texts and
manuscripts. The 'movement' was epitomised by the Latin
tag, *ad fontes* – back to the beginning, the source, the origin.
It was about authenticity and authority. Its tools were the
mastery of languages and textual scholarship. Humanists
were editors of texts. Such skills were readily acquired in the
universities and scholarly circles of sixteenth-century Europe
as patrons and faculties eagerly adopted the new fashion.
They were also readily transferable from secular to sacred
texts. Calvin's biblical commentaries are as much a tribute to
his humanist education as to his theological perception.

The unwitting godfather of the Reformed tradition is
therefore Erasmus, that droll, witty, peripatetic humanist. His
rapier thrusts of wit which exposed the foibles and weaknesses of the Church, his passion for scholarship and precision, his lofty transcendentalism, and his clearing of the
barnacles of scholastic accretions from the pristine beauty of
Greek New Testament words all helped to shape Reformed
minds and methods. Zwingli worshipped at the shrine and
Calvin had thoroughly imbibed the humanist agenda before he
arrived in Geneva.[11] His first published work was an exemp-
lary humanist exercise, an edition of Seneca's *De Clementia*.
The Swiss Reformation was shaped by humanism. The Swiss
Reformers shared Luther's passion for engagement with the
text of Scripture, but whereas Luther's primary theological
concern was with the nature of forgiveness, the Swiss wanted
to know if there was a word from God, and if there was, what
the implications were for the ordering of human society.
Theirs was a religion of the book, a journey back to the

beginnings, to origins and authority, to the words of Scripture in Greek and Hebrew. Whilst Luther and his followers were content that only that which was forbidden by Scripture should be excluded from the Church, the Reformed insisted that only that which had scriptural warrant was permissible.

By the time Zwingli met his untimely death in the battle against the Catholic cantons in 1531, the main contours of Reformed spirituality were already becoming clear. The landscape was defined by Scripture. Simplicity and clarity were touchstones, and understanding, and therefore education, were highly prized. This was a spiritual tradition in which words and their meanings mattered. Indeed, Reformed worship at its worst can still be mistaken for an Open University broadcast!

Heinrich Bullinger (1504–75) was 27 when he succeeded Zwingli. His inheritance was unpromising. The alliance of the Swiss Reformed cities with their German evangelical cousins to the north lay dead on the battlefield alongside Zwingli's butchered body, and next to it lay any possibility of unifying the cantons and cities of Switzerland under the banner of Reformed Christianity. However, Bullinger was an exceptional man: wise, patient, the father of 11 children, a singular preacher and a profound and original theologian in his own right. An eirenic, ecumenically minded leader, he sought friendship and unity within the Reformed and Protestant world through copious correspondence over four decades (over 12,000 of his letters survive). In this he met with limited but conspicuous success. In 1549 he was instrumental in creating eucharistic agreement between Zurich and Geneva in the Concensus Tigurinus, and he was the principal author of the Second Helvetic Confession (1566), which was eventually to be accepted as a definitive statement of Reformed theology by the Swiss cantons, the Palatinate, France (1571), Hungary (1567), Poland (1571 and 1578) and Scotland (1566). He was also the first Reformed thinker to give systematic attention to covenant theology, which was to loom large in the Reformed consciousness in the seventeenth century.

It has sometimes been said that baptism was the Achilles' heel of the Reformation. If, as Zwingli believed, only practices warranted by Scripture were permissible, what was one to make of infant baptism? Anabaptist radicals, those who looked for another, believer's, baptism, were rife in Zurich. It was whilst he was defending infant baptism that Zwingli first took up the idea of covenant. If circumcision symbolised God's covenant with Israel in Genesis 17, then baptism was the symbol of God's covenant with the new Israel. Covenant, *Bund* in German, had an immediate appeal to the Swiss, for their independent cantons and cities were held together by a series of covenants. Zwingli clutched at the idea with polemical enthusiasm, but it was Bullinger who made it the lynch-pin of a theological system. He tried to explain his thinking to his fiancée Anna in a letter of 24 February 1528:

> the Old Testament begins with the covenant which God struck with Abraham and in him with all His faithful ones, so that He alone would be the single good, the treasure of all goods, on whom alone we should depend and before whom we should walk with integrity ... No new covenant was established in the New Testament; rather, it only demonstrates irrefutably that God wants to be our God, that is, our good and sufficiency.[12]

Covenant theology takes the whole of God's encounter with humanity seriously. It holds creation and redemption, Israel and the Church, the world and the Church within one narrative, the story of God's love for human beings. It moves through Scripture by way of Adam, Noah, Abraham, Moses, Jeremiah and Jesus, to name but a few. Biblical pictures of the covenant provided Reformed thinkers with rich and imaginative soil. Bullinger understood the whole of history to be operating within the covenant made with the seed of Adam (Gen. 3:15). God's love encompassed all. Although not a universalist as we would understand the term in modern theology, Bullinger was graciously reticent before the ambiguity of

Scripture, refusing to make neat hospital corners out of the ragged edges of the sheets of the story of salvation.

The covenant between God and humanity was for Bullinger a bilateral one. It was not just God who had responsibilities. Human beings had them too. The law of God, which Bullinger believed could be summarised in the greatest commandment – love God and your neighbour – was binding. Because the covenant included all, it was impossible to be outside the commonwealth, and therefore the law of God applied to all. Law was in this sense very significant for the Reformed, because it enabled them to solve the Lutheran paradox of how to persuade people to be moral beings if they were justified by faith (and therefore did not need to live good lives to merit salvation).

J. Wayne Baker has called this the 'other' Reformed tradition, for Zurich had a formidable foil, Geneva, and her preoccupations would soon predominate. Covenant theology would recur, some two generations later, but then it would be snared in the fine mesh of the machinations of the so-called federal theologians who preferred the language of covenants of work and grace to talk of old and new covenants, and the manipulation of a dry, scholastic system to the fearless engagement with Scripture which was the mark of the first generations of Reformed thinkers. In the meantime Bullinger found himself in dialogue and occasional dispute with the greatest of classical Reformed theologians, John Calvin (1509–64).

Calvin and Geneva

Calvin is a complex figure. Born in France, educated as a lawyer, deeply influenced by humanism, he spent his working life as a religious exile. A chance encounter with Guillaume Farel (1489–1565) as he was passing through Geneva in 1536 was to yoke his fortunes to the city in an uneasy relationship until his death in 1564. Calvin had envisaged a life for himself as a wandering scholar and writer. He did not consider himself pastorally gifted, but he was shocked by the fiery Farel's argument that the needs of the Genevan Reformation were so great that God would curse his tranquillity if he refused to stay and help. However, he agreed to do so as a 'doctor' or reader of Scripture, not as a pastor.[13]

The pair of them were thrown out in 1538. Calvin accepted an invitation from Martin Bucer (1491–1551) to join him in Strasbourg as pastor to the French refugee congregation. During three singularly happy years Calvin combined scholarly and pastoral pursuits and married Idette de Bure, a widow with two children. Never one to parade his emotions, it is easy to underestimate the impact of the death of their three children in infancy, and then of Idette herself in 1549. His was a spirituality that had a depth and robustness which could absorb and manage the 'commonplace' tragedies of the sixteenth century.

That spirituality was worked out primarily in Geneva, for he accepted a request to return there in 1541. The prospect frightened him: 'Rather would I submit to a hundred other deaths than to that cross on which one must perish daily a thousand times', he wrote to Farel.[14] However, persuaded by Bucer, he went and remained as 'Moderator of the Company of Pastors' until his death. The relationship between the 'secular' powers and the Church was critical in the cities and cantons of the Swiss Reformation, for no one was outside the covenant, and the law of God was the foundation of civil as well as ecclesiastical law. Despite the adoption of the *Ecclesiastical Ordinances* by the city council in November 1541, Geneva was never easy. The degree of regulation which Calvin thought was a mark of a godly commonwealth was resented, as were the waves of religious refugees whose presence threatened settled power structures. Calvin's language reflects the turmoil – the Church is like the ark tossed in the deluge. Matters reached a climax in the mid 1550s. Thereafter Calvin's position was moderately secure, but he did not accept Genevan citizenship until 1559.

Primarily a preacher and teacher, his influence was felt

throughout Protestant Europe, through extensive correspondence and a voluminous output of sermons (he preached something like 4000 sermons after his return to Geneva, over 170 a year), commentaries, theological essays, and one of the great works of Christian thought, his *Institutes of the Christian Religion*, which went through several editions before achieving its final shape in 1559. All that was fitted into the demanding working life of a minister, which Calvin took with the utmost seriousness. He was a driven man.

The heart of Calvin's theology and spirituality is the mystical union between Christ and the believer. That was primarily a corporate experience. Calvin had a remarkably high doctrine of the Church, so the union between the believer and Christ is given expression in baptism, which is reception into God's people. Within the Church believers are given everything that Jesus Christ has and is, through the preaching of the Word, the administration of the sacraments and the liturgical life of the Church. That in turn prepares us for obedient service to God in the world. So, for Calvin, being in Christ has two results which are closely related. First, it means living in a proper relationship with God. Second, it should result in growth in grace and a tangible life of discipleship. In other words, a moral life.[15]

Reformed spirituality was a recapturing of the transcendence and awesomeness of God. Few have articulated that more profoundly and systematically than Calvin. He is insistent that human beings cannot know God. God cannot be encompassed by human reason, so speculative theology and philosophy can have no place in the spiritual life. Reflecting on theological disputes, he wrote:

> There are some ... who would like in their disputes always to draw conclusions in the fashion of the philosophers, that everything should be put in order so that there should be no diversity at all and there should be agreement everywhere; but such people have never known what it is to be touched by God ...[16]

To be touched by God, to experience but not know his transcendence, was to encounter gentleness and love. If Calvin
understood God's holiness, he also had an instinctive awareness of God's tenderness. He told his Genevan congregation,
'Our Lord makes himself uniquely familiar; he is like a nurse,
like a mother; he does not compare himself only to fathers, who
are so benign and humane toward their children, but he says
that he is more than mother, more than nurse.' And again, 'Let
us not be deterred from coming to him [God] by any dread or
doubt; for what more could he do than when he stooped down
as if he were a hen, so that his majesty would no longer be
terrible to us and would not appal us.'[17] God, the nurse, the
mother, the hen; any account of Calvin's spirituality needs to
allow those images of love to stand in tension with his awed
appreciation of God's power.

Calvin had a profound awareness of the love of God. He
wrote movingly of the everyday miracle of birth, awestruck
how God 'by his secret and incomprehensible power' kept
the foetus alive in the womb. He saw every moment of life
encompassed by the providence of God, because providence
was what made God's love efficacious.[18] And it is but a small,
if scriptural, step from there to a theology of predestination.
He developed this theology to bring comfort, not fear. He
knew it to be a mystery, an abyss, a labyrinth. He knew it to
be dangerous and scandalous, and the only reason he ventured there was because (like Paul and Augustine before
him) he found it in Scripture. The tragedy for the Reformed
tradition is that some who proudly called themselves Calvinist did not exercise his reticence.

Calvin's influence spread across the Reformed world. It was
a world held together by the *lingua franca* of Latin which
enabled the rapid exchange of scholarly ideas. It was also,
tragically, a world turned upside down by religious revolution, full of refugees, many of whom made their way to
Geneva, staying there for a few months or years before
carrying Calvin's ideas back with them.

The Reformed were from the first catholic. Theirs was not a

programme designed to antagonise or destroy. It was rather
motivated by a passion for reform, for a return to what the
Church was meant to be. That was why Heinrich Bullinger
prefaced his *Decades* (1552) – 50 sermons which he believed
captured the essence of Christianity – with a chapter which
affirmed the first four ecumenical councils, eleven creeds of
the ancient Church and an imperial decree for the catholic
faith. Calvin likewise affirmed the first four councils and
structured his *Institutes* on the Apostles' Creed. Possibly the
finest patristic scholar of his age, his indebtedness to the
Fathers, particularly Cyprian, Chrysostom and Augustine, is
clear in every page of his writings. However, by the time
Calvin died, it was clear that unity was an impossible dream,
even amongst Protestants. Pluralism was the Reformation's
sorry legacy. That was to be worked out as nationalism and
religion fused with unholy violence in the Wars of Religion,
and in the development of ever hardening confessional
boundaries.

The expansion of the Reformed world and the development of 'federal' theology

The Reformed world expanded rapidly. By 1600 there was a
Reformed presence in France, the Netherlands, Scotland, the
Palatinate, Bohemia, Poland (briefly) and Hungary. Some
were majority churches, others minority. Most adhered to a
presbyterian structure – that is to say, government by the
presbyterate in council. Calvin was a fine, if pragmatic,
ecclesiologist.

Whereas the first Reformed churches in Switzerland were
created by the fiat of government, in France they were
minority churches in a majority culture, subject to persecution from their foundation until in 1598 Henry IV granted
them freedom of conscience in the Edict of Nantes. This
broadening of Reformed experience to include both 'state
religion' and 'dissent' would later bear fruit in a spirituality
that both protected the rights of the Church and understood

political and social activism to be essential constituents of Christian discipleship.

A little further north, in the Netherlands, the Reformed movement was synonymous with the northern provinces' struggle for freedom from the Spanish (1568–1648). Across the North Sea the tentacles of Genevan Calvinism wound themselves around the Scottish soul, thanks to the fiery passions of John Knox (1505–72), who was himself twice exiled to Geneva before becoming the architect of the Scottish Reformation of 1560.

Germany remained Lutheran territory, despite brief Reformed flourishings in Strasbourg and Hesse. Reformed theologians were more welcome in the Palatinate, and the University of Heidelberg became a veritable centre of Reformed activity in the late sixteenth century, attracting scholars of the calibre of Ursinus and Erastus. To the east, Poland fell under Reformed influence during Calvin's day, but this was reversed some years later by the dynamic resurgence of Catholicism. In Bohemia the Reformation was built on Hussite foundations. Most of the region became Lutheran, but a Reformed influence still exists today in Slovakia and the Czech Republic. In neighbouring Hungary Reformed theology and nationalist revolt merged, and the Church there adopted an episcopal polity in jurisdiction, not status.[19]

The 80 years between the final edition of Calvin's *Institutes* of 1559 and the Westminster Confession of 1647 saw the hot lava of the first generation of the Reformations flow down the volcano and form set contours which would determine the Reformed spiritual landscape for future generations. Three processes can be identified. First, the composition of confessions of faith became increasingly important. Confessions had their origins in the theological disputations which marked the first years of the Reformations. Works like Zwingli's '67 theses' (1523) were intellectual warm-up exercises for these gruelling academic contests. Then there was also a need to explain the principles of reformation both to believers and opponents. The First Helvetic Confession (1536) is a good example of that impulse. It was an apologetical method which was congenial to the Reformed mind, rational, biblical and systematic, yet also provisional. Unlike other confessional bodies, the Reformed never made one confession mandatory. Some, like the Heidelberg Confession and the Second Helvetic Confession, gained lasting respect.

Secondly, the courageous, even thrilling, encounter with Scripture which had crafted the first generation of the Reformations was replaced by an intricate scholasticism known as 'federal theology', of which the Westminster Confession is a fine example. Grace was almost but not quite made subordinate to law.

Foedus was a Latin translation of the Hebrew word for 'covenant', *berith*,[20] so federal theology is a form of covenant theology. Covenant is one of the great themes of Scripture: God makes a covenant with Noah and signs it with a rainbow; God calls Abraham out, shows him the night sky and promises that his descendants shall be more numerous than the stars; and one day, says Jeremiah, there will be a new covenant, written in our hearts. This wine, says Jesus, is the new covenant in my blood. All theologies are therefore in some sense covenant theologies, for they all deal with the subject-matter of the promises of God. Calvin, indeed, was a covenant theologian in that sense. Federal theology, as represented by the Westminster Confession, made the covenant the determining principle of its theological schema. It did so by speaking of a covenant of works and a covenant of grace. Chapter VII of the Westminster Confession states: 'The first covenant made with Man, was a Covenant of Works, wherein Life was promised to Adam, and to him in his Posterity; upon Condition of perfect and personal Obedience.'

So, the relationship between human beings and God is from the start a legal one. Obedience to God is laid upon us, and Christ becomes the perfectly obedient second Adam who keeps the covenant of works. So, the covenant of grace is really the covenant of works in disguise.[21]

Federal theology has many strengths. It takes creation seriously. It encompasses the whole of humanity, and thus provides the basis for a proper theology of the state. But it has significant weaknesses. It can all too easily subordinate grace to law, discipleship to morality, and reduce divine mystery to human systems. It is a rich irony that it should be termed 'Calvinist', for of all the Reformers, Calvin was the most acutely aware of the mystery of God, in the union of Christ and believer, in the eucharistic feast, and in the dark and dangerous labyrinths of election.

Third, Reformed church order became defined. Calvin was a pragmatic and open ecclesiologist. He was clear that the marks of the true Church were the preaching of the Word and the administration of the sacraments. He admitted that those marks could be found in a variety of church orders, and he was refreshingly relaxed about non-essentials, such 'things indifferent' as vestments and bishops. Like all six-teenth-century Reformers, he sought a model for church order in the New Testament, and believed that he found there the government of the church by presbyters. However, once the episcopate had been decisively rejected, he felt his way towards a new way of being church and experimented and borrowed. His concept of the eldership (lay officers charged with overseeing the moral welfare of the community) was adapted from what he had observed in Bucer's Stras-bourg,[22] but there was a fluidity about his practice and advice. His successors, particularly Andrew Melville (1545–1622) in the *Second Book of Discipline* (1578), set the elder-ship in concrete. It became a defining characteristic of Reformed ecclesiology. Calvinism was becoming Presbyteri-anism.

However, the prevailing orthodoxy did not find itself unchallenged. Reformed theology was at heart an ordering of Scripture, standing under the judgement of Scripture. Reformed theologians knew better than to accept second-order confessions without returning to Scripture.

Jacob Arminius, Dutch independence, and predestination

The Low Countries (roughly modern Belgium and the Netherlands) were, in the Middle Ages, a series of counties, duchies and dioceses which belonged to the Duke of Burgundy and the Holy Roman Empire. They were united under Hapsburg rule in the sixteenth century. In 1555 the Holy Roman Emperor, Charles V, granted control of Spain and the Low Countries to his son, Philip II. Calvinism had first been established in the Walloon-speaking areas of the south and south-west (Walloon is a dialect of French). In 1561 these churches produced the Belgic Confession, a translation of the French Confession of 1559. The Hapsburgs had reacted to early displays of Protestant sympathy with efficient severity. However, in the 1550s Reformed Protestantism revived, thanks to help from exilic refugee communities like the ones in London and Emden, and that revival intensified in the 1560s.

In 1566, the so-called 'wonder year' of Protestant success, the edicts against heresy were moderated on the demand of the nobles, and field preaching broke out around Amsterdam, heralding the emergence of an indigenous Reformation, reliant on the Heidelberg Confession rather than the Belgic Confession, and iconoclastic rioting spread across the province. Control was slipping. This was revolt, and Philip dispatched the Duke of Alva with a large army to sort it out. Alva extracted terrible revenge, which simply strengthened Dutch resolve, and they continued their battle for independence under the leadership of William of Orange until he was assassinated in 1584, and then under his son, Prince Maurice.

The centre of gravity of Dutch Protestantism and the impetus for independence moved northwards in the 1570s, resulting in the Union of Utrecht in 1579 which united the northern provinces and some southern territories into what would eventually become the Netherlands (those which did not join became what is now Belgium).

Jacob Arminius's life (1560–1609) coincided with these turbulent years and the fight for independence. His theology and the early history of his nation fused together in a complex and sometimes bewildering web. He was born in Oudewater in Utrecht. His father died whilst he was a small child and he was brought up in poor circumstances by his widowed mother. When he was 15, Oudewater took the decision to side with William the Silent, national independence and Protestantism. Spanish troops descended on the rebellious town, and most of Arminius's family were massacred.[23]

Somehow means were raised for him to study at the new Protestant university of Leiden, where he proved an exceptional pupil. He left in 1581. The new Protestant government of Amsterdam (the 'Alteration' of 1578 marked the switch from Catholicism to Protestantism in the city) agreed to fund his further studies in Geneva, in return for a signed agreement that thereafter he would serve the church of Amsterdam. So it was that Arminius found himself a pupil of the great de Bèze, and after that he became a minister in Amsterdam.

By that time the revolt had succeeded. The seven northern provinces formed the Union of Utrecht in 1579 and declared their independence in 1581. Arminius became an adopted Amsterdammer, accepted as a kindred soul by the Calvinist merchant establishment which had brought about the Alteration, and in 1590 he became part of that élite by his marriage to Lijsbet Raeal. She was the daughter of Laurens Raeal, one of the leading merchant-Reformers, a cultured poet and song-writer, who promoted Dutch literature as part of national independence.[24]

Arminius was a scholarly preacher, a Reformed theologian who refused to let any secondary authority come between him and Scripture. As he preached on Paul, particularly on Romans 7 and 9, he became increasingly dissatisfied with de Bèze's treatment of predestination, and aroused the suspicions of his colleagues. However, nothing was ever proved against him, and he retained the wholehearted support of the city council. In 1603 he was called to the chair of theology at Leiden, and remained there until his death six years later. They were to be years of unremitting controversy. It is hard to anatomise the debate, conducted as it was in the minutiae of Calvinistic scholasticism, for Arminius never actually denied the doctrine of predestination. However, he did question its centrality in Calvinist theology, argued eloquently against the irresistibility of the grace of God, and fought (unsuccessfully) for the revision of the two basic documents of Dutch Calvinism – the Belgic and Heidelberg Confessions.

Predestination (as opposed to election) was the soft underbelly of Reformed thought, for although traces of the doctrine can be found in Scripture (e.g. Rom. 8:20, 29–30; Eph. 1:3–4), it owes more to Augustine's systematising genius than to St Paul. It was therefore unsurprising that the first major challenge to Reformed orthodoxy concentrated on this doctrine's perceived shortcomings. It had long been a matter of debate. As early as 1551 the ex-Carmelite friar, Jérôme Bolsec, had taken Calvin to task on the matter in an audacious lecture before the Company of Pastors in Geneva. Calvin was at least willing to be reticent in the face of what he perceived to be the divine mystery of predestination. His followers and pupils, forced to define themselves more sharply by debates with Lutherans in particular, hardened mystery into dogma. Most prominently, Calvin's successor at Geneva, Theodore de Bèze, developed a sophisticated supralapsarian understanding, which stated that God had worked out who would and would not be saved even before Eve's hand had reached for the apple.

Arminius was the theological incarnation of old Amsterdam: tolerant, convinced of the need for a plurality of confessions rather than the constrictions of one, a defender of liberty of conscience. But Amsterdam, and indeed the Netherlands, was changing. Spanish persecution had resulted in immigration of a stricter breed of Calvinist from the south. The Reformed church, the symbol of independence, had only been established for 40 years. To be seen to attack it was to be mistaken for attacking independence itself, especially if you chose the same target (predestination) as such eloquent Catholic critics as Robert Bellarmine. That was Arminius's political tragedy. Theologically, he was eventually to win the war, for by the end of the nineteenth century most Reformed churches modified their understandings of predestination in ways which Arminius would have considered too radical.

Theology and politics were inextricably intertwined in the aftermath of his death. The two strands of the Dutch Reformation, Calvinism and liberty, clashed grievously. Elsewhere in Europe Reformation led to religious uniformity (*cuius regio, eius religio*), but in the Netherlands it produced a religiously plural state. The Reformed Church was granted official status. It took over the buildings and the income of the Catholic Church, but citizens were not required to be in membership of the new church. Indeed, the Reformed remained an influential minority until well into the seventeenth century. Government, both local and provincial, was as concerned with liberty as with theology. Arminius was a member of that governing élite, a Hollander rooted in traditions of indigenous dissent. His main opponent and fellow professor at Leiden, Franciscus Gomarus (1563–1641), was from Brugge, a hard-line Calvinist exile. They represented the clash of two cultures. Arminius and his followers (the Remonstrants) were, in essence, arguing for a Church for everyone, whereas Gomarus and his party (the Contra-Remonstrants) were looking for a gathered Church of the saints.[25]

The year after Arminius died, his followers presented a Remonstance to the States-General of the United Provinces. The theological question at the centre of the debate – could the grace of God be resisted? – was rapidly eclipsed by the political question of where the balance of power lay between Church and State. The Remonstrants were committed Erastians, so it was unsurprising that the governing élite favoured their cause. Chief amongst them was the political architect of Dutch independence, the lawyer Johan Oldenbarneveldt

(1547–1619). In 1609 Oldenbarneveldt had concluded a 12-year truce with the Spanish. To his opponents it looked as if he had simply licensed the Spanish to attack at their convenience, admitted the loss of the southern provinces, and therefore betrayed the immigrant Calvinists of the north. The truce intensified a split with Prince Maurice of Nassau (son of the great liberator William the Silent), who favoured a continuation of the military struggle. It did not take long for an alliance to be formed between Maurice and the Calvinist Contra-Remonstrants. True nationalism meant belonging to the war party and adhering to strict Calvinism.

The Remonstrance was signed by forty-four ministers. It contained five points: that God's decrees of election and reprobation were conditional on God's foreknowledge of faith; that Christ died for all, although the forgiveness of sin was enjoyed by none except believers; that regeneration by the Spirit is a prerequisite of salvation; that grace is resistible; that the perseverance of the saints can be neither denied nor asserted.

A long and bitter struggle ensued. Thanks to their support in the magistracy, Remonstrants held on to power in many Dutch cities until, in 1618, Maurice used his armed forces to occupy the towns and replace the magistrates with Contra-Remonstrants. They then called the long-awaited national Synod, at Dordrecht (Dort). It was international, including twenty-six delegates from abroad, and it met for six months between November 1618 and May 1619. The result was a swingeing defeat for Arminianism. Remonstrants were banned from pulpits on pain of banishment. Some, including the great jurist Hugo Grotius (1583–1641), were imprisoned. Grotius escaped in a book-box after three years. Jan van Oldenbarneveldt, aged 71, having served as Grand Pensionary for 33 years, was judicially murdered days after the end of the Synod. It was a sad, miserable day in Dutch history.

The rulings of the Synod (accepted by all the Reformed churches of Europe, including the Church of England) are commonly summarised by the acronym TULIP: the total depravity of human nature; God's unconditional decree of election; limited atonement (for the elect only); the irresistibility of God's grace; and the perseverance of the saints. In other words, it upheld the orthodoxy of Reformed scholasticism, and protected God's freedom and sovereignty, but at the cost of God's love.

The English Reformation and the Reformed

The second major challenge to Reformed orthodoxy was ecclesiological, and it arose in England. The process of reform in England was long and complex. Theology and politics were inextricably entwined. Although Henry VIII's initial break with Rome did little to change the theological and spiritual disposition of the nation, the reigns of his three children were a roller-coaster ride towards a redefined spirituality. Edward VI (1547–53) carried out a reforming *blitzkrieg* of Swiss intensity. Gone in one fell swoop were the Mass, images, prayers for the dead and a matrix of concepts that held past, present and future in equilibrium. His half-sister Mary (1553–58), the holiest and devoutest of monarchs, sought to restore the Catholic faith, but died of cancer before the programme was fully formed. Her half-sister Elizabeth (1558–1603) came to the throne determined to restore balance and steer a median course between the Scylla of Rome and the Charybdis of Geneva. She did so with verve, style and authority, ensuring that the monarch remained the supreme governor of the Church of England, maintaining the episcopate, accepting limited liturgical reform and crushing reformers who ventured too noisily into public debate.

However, some were bold enough to argue that further reform was essential in the Church of England. Many had first-hand experience of Reformed Europe (including Presbyterian Scotland). Like their European fellow travellers, they regarded Scripture as their ultimate authority. They were not willing to trade the Word of God for political advantage, and the pressure points were debates about the nature of episcopacy, and (above all) liturgy. They became known as Puritans. For the most part they kept their debate within the structures of the Church, pressing for change from within. However, some felt called to reject the established Church as corrupt and ungodly, and advocate a new order. These separatists, most notably Robert Browne (1540–1630), John Greenwood (c. 1560–93), Henry Barrow (c.1550–93) and John Penry (1562/3–93), argued that the local church, the local gathering of the saints, was the true authority in the life of the Church. They were cruelly repressed because they represented a threat to the established political order. Greenwood, Barrow and Penry were hanged in 1593.

Separatism, or as it later became known, independency or congregationalism, was to become a minor theme in the English historical symphony after 1662, and a major theme in American history as early practitioners sought freedom in the new world. Although ecclesiologically divergent from the Reformed tradition, separatists were in theological continuity with it, Calvinists to a man and a woman.

Elizabeth maintained the unity of the Church of England, managing its tensions with singular skill. However, Puritanism refused to go away, however robust the management, and it became a significant ingredient in the collapse of the country into Civil War in 1640. In 1642 Parliament turned its attention to the reform of the Church and the abolition of episcopacy. It called an Assembly in 1643, consisting of 20 members each of the Upper House and the House of Commons and 121 clergy of varying persuasions. Meeting in Westminster, their productions all bear that name – the Westminster Directory (1645) which set out a pattern (not a liturgy) for worship, the Westminster Confession (1647) and the Shorter and Longer Catechisms (1648). It is a nice irony that the Westminster Confession, perhaps the best known of all Reformed confessions, was written for an English Reformed Church which never came into being, but was adopted by the Church of Scotland in 1647 as its confessional basis.

The Westminster documents were eloquent, clear and uncompromising statements of Reformed orthodoxy. The Assembly's commitment to double predestination and covenant theology was unequivocal. They represent a high-point of Reformed self-confidence, a blue-print for an alternative English Church and spirituality which was never to emerge from the incompetent muddle of the English Republic. Less than a generation later (1660) the experiment was at an end, and a sharper-edged, more clearly defined, less inclusive Church of England was to force the English Reformed tradition into the margins of history.

The Reformed from 1600 to 2000

Intolerance and persecution in the seventeenth century forced Reformed Christians into waves of migration. English Puritans sought freedom in the new world, founding Plymouth Colony in 1620 and the Massachusetts Bay Colony. Huguenots settled in Florida in 1562. The Dutch founded New Amsterdam (later New York) in 1624. By the beginning of the eighteenth century organised Reformed churches were being created in America. The first presbytery of Philadelphia was founded under the influence of Francis Makemie in 1706 – growing rapidly (thanks to immigration) into the Synod of Philadelphia, with three presbyteries – Philadelphia, New Castle and Long Island – in 1716. The Synod was to adopt the Westminster Confession in 1729, but allowed for 'scrupling' (disagreement), particularly about Westminster's perception of the role of the civil magistrate in the American colonies. America was to become a fascinating melting pot of European cultures. Christians of most traditions were represented amongst the immigrants, and those from a Reformed background were particularly influential in the colonisation process. However, they did not form one Reformed church but maintained their separate 'national' identities and traditions.

Whilst emigration westwards was carrying the Reformed way of living to America, the success of the Catholic Church's reformation was transforming its fortunes in parts of Europe. During the seventeenth century the reimposition of Catholicism in Hungary was accompanied by repressive measures which led in the end to the 'Bloody tribunal' of Bratislava in 1673, and many Reformed pastors were sold as galley slaves. In France, the revocation of the Edict of Nantes (1685) by Louis XIV led to the mass migration of over 200,000 Huguenots. They settled across Europe, and some found their way to other continents, including some to South Africa. Their experience of what it meant to be a minority Reformed church lent a certain steel to their understanding of Reformed discipleship.

Arminius's career in the Netherlands coincided with the rise to international significance of Dutch trade and expansion. Indeed, one of his most implacable opponents in Amsterdam, Petrus Plancius (1522–1622), was as much famed as a cartographer and scientist as a theologian. His first map had been of biblical lands, but later works showed good routes to the East and West Indies, Africa and China. He seems to have obtained privileged Portuguese information (no one knows how!) and used it to good effect. At precisely the time that he was engaging in theological disputes with Arminius in 1593, he was also hatching plans with three merchant neighbours to exploit this knowledge in sea voyages.[26] Those first tentative steps led to the launching of the Dutch East India Company in 1602 and the establishment of a Dutch empire. In its wake Reformed churches, initially largely expatriate, were formed in the Caribbean, North Brazil, South Africa, Sri Lanka and Taiwan.

Reformed scholasticism reached its heights in the great confessions of the seventeenth century, but most especially the Westminster Confession (1647) and its related documents, which were to have definitive influence in Scotland and America. However, within a century that bastion of security was under attack. The contrasting yet complementary forces of eighteenth-century religious life, the Enlightenment and the Evangelical Revival, were both to raise profound questions for the Reformed churches and result in their transformation in the nineteenth century.

Reformed theologians were innately suspicious of reason. Humans were fallen. They were therefore convinced that reason could not lead people to God. It was deeply flawed, to be distrusted. Enlightenment thinkers, conversely, were convinced of the centrality of human reason and made it the measure of all doctrine. In their eyes, reliance on revelation would not do. Equally, the new leaders of the Evangelical revival which swept across Europe and America looked for the proof of faith in the movement of the human soul. Acceptance of the doctrine of justification by faith had to be accompanied by the 'proof' of individual conversion. Calvin would have been appalled.

These intertwining forces helped to bring a new Reformed theology and spirituality to birth. Within a generation of the last reiteration of Reformed orthodoxy, the *Formula Concensus Helvetica* (1675), Reformed theologians were seeking ways to reconcile reason and revelation. The most exciting and beautiful work was done in America as Jonathan Edwards (1703–58) sought to fuse the God of Scripture, the ordered world of Isaac Newton and the deeps of the revivalist soul in a new Calvinist-inspired synthesis. Edwards, who remains one of the greatest of Reformed theologians, still managed to operate within the broad structures of traditional Reformed thought.

Ten years after Edwards' untimely death, Friedrich Schleiermacher (1768–1834) was born in Silesia. He became the Reformed preacher at the Charité in Berlin (1798), and was later to hold theological chairs at Halle and Berlin. Schleiermacher was a theological genius. Almost single-handedly he showed how theology could be transposed into the intellectual key of the Enlightenment. In a world that places the limits of understanding at the edges of experience, Schleiermacher developed a systematic understanding of Christian teaching as the fullest expression of religious experience, which was itself the profoundest form of human experience. His influence was to be considerable. The English-speaking world did not fully appreciate him until the early years of the twentieth century when John Oman (1860–1939), the Principal of the Presbyterian Westminster College, Cambridge, provided translations of *The Christian Faith* and *Speeches on Religion to Its Cultural Despisers*. Schleiermacher is therefore the *éminence grise* behind the development of twentieth-century liberal theology.

By the mid nineteenth century the Reformed were no longer simply a European phenomenon. Colonialism and the beginnings of world travel meant that Reformed churches were to be found on every continent. Each has its own history, its own distinctive story of interaction, of shaping and being shaped by its context. The seeds were being sown for the shift of gravity from Europe and the West to the South and the East which is such a distinctive factor in contemporary Reformed life. However, there is no doubt that European and American Reformed experience moulded the shape of the Reformed family between 1850 and 1950.

The first contour was provided by theology. Confessional statements like the Westminster Confession and the Second Helvetic Confession were subject to investigation, criticism, modification and in some cases rejection. Churches and theologians found themselves caught up in an exciting and frightening ferment as they sought to reconcile revelation and reason, and provide a coherent account of the faith that was in them for a post-Enlightenment age. The Reformed began to rediscover their theological plurality, and to cope with both the liberation and the pain that engendered. The development of liberalism was countered by the explosion of neo-orthodoxy, or dialectical theology, after the First World War. Karl Barth (1886–1968), himself Swiss Reformed, was the towering figure of the movement, refashioning theology in the face of God's majesty and otherness, rediscovering the power of both Scripture and the Reformers, proclaiming once more God's initiative in salvation.

The potential of Barthian neo-orthodoxy became clear in

Barth's drafting of the Barmen Declaration of 1934 which determinedly opposed Nazi ideology and led to the formation of the Confessing Church. The Reformed realised that the age of confessions was not past. It remained a legitimate way of doing theology, and has reappeared more recently in defining opposition to the apartheid system in South Africa and the injustices of the world economic system.[27]

The second contour was provided by the international explosion of missionary societies between 1790 and 1850 – the London Missionary Society (1795), the Nederlandsch Zendelinggenootschap (1797), the South Africa Mission Society (1799), the American Board of Commissioners for Foreign Mission (1810), the Basel Mission (1835), to name just some of the most prominent ones – and the consequent practice of mission. This broadened the internationalism of the Reformed family. Historians of missions have shown how difficult it is to disentangle religious motives from colonial ideals and ideas. The legacy of the missionary movement is ambiguous, yet at its best Reformed mission was acutely aware of the radical challenge of the Gospel to the structures of colonialism. A misunderstanding of Reformed theology might well have bolstered the ideology of apartheid in South Africa. However, that must be balanced by an honourable tradition of LMS missionaries who fought for native rights, from John Philip in the 1820s and 1830s to those who stood courageously against apartheid in the 1950s and 1960s.

The theological legacy of the missionary movement brought to the fore questions of the relationship between Christianity and the other world faiths and Christ and indigenous culture, as well as the sustained reflection of the churches of the post-colonial South. These form major agenda items for the world-wide Reformed family.

The third contour is a commitment to ecumenism. Ecumenism's roots are to be found in Jesus' prayer in John 17 'that they may all be one'. If that was one parent of the modern ecumenical movement, the other was a growing perception of the scandal of the disunity and fragmentation of the world Church made real by international travel and the growth of the missionary movement. The Reformed were amongst the founders of modern ecumenism. In 1841 a Swiss theologian called Philip Schaff moved to the little German Reformed seminary at Mercersberg (Pennsylvania) from the University of Berlin. An indomitably energetic church historian and biblical scholar, he cast a critical eye over the American Christian scene, dryly criticising the sectarian mentality and the ideal of religious liberty which placed no limits on the multiplication and institutionalisation of religious lunacy. He preached rather of a realm 'where there shall be no Europe, no America, no Catholicism and Protestantism, but an undivided Kingdom of God.'[28] Schaff's ecumenical commitment was seen in his support of the foundation of the Evangelical Alliance in 1846, and his energetic advocacy of the creation of the World Alliance of Reformed Churches in 1875.

These bodies were in some ways precursors of the ecumenical movement which developed after the 1910 Edinburgh Missionary Conference, eventually resulting in the World Council of Churches. The first two General Secretaries of the Council were both from Reformed churches – Willem A. Visser 't Hooft (1948–66) from the Netherlands Reformed Church and Eugene Blake (1966–72) from the United Presbyterian Church in the USA. About a third of the first members of the Council were Reformed, Presbyterian and Congregational churches.

However, not all Reformed churches welcomed this development. A number, mainly of Dutch extraction and deeply committed to the classical confessions, created the Reformed Ecumenical Synod in 1946. On the fundamentalist wing, the International Council of Christian Churches was founded by Carl McIntire in 1948, denouncing the ecumenical movement as apostate and heretical.

However, the movement towards unity gathered pace during the 1960s and 1970s. The most significant ecumenical event in the twentieth century was the Second Vatican

Council (1962–65). It saw Catholicism adopt many of the reforms which were central to the Reformers of the sixteenth century – the use of vernacular languages in the liturgy, regular preaching of the Word, eucharistic celebration using both bread and wine. It also saw the beginning of Roman Catholicism's genuine engagement with the ecumenical movement, and serious engagement with partners on some of the central theological causes of division, like justification by faith. It is difficult to overestimate the importance of the joint declaration on justification with the Lutherans of 1999 which 'encompass[es] a consensus on basic truths of the doctrine of justification and shows that the remaining differences in its explication are no longer the occasion for doctrinal condemnations.'[29] This in turn has led many Reformed churches to modify the anti-Catholicism of some of their confessions, and ask seriously whether they should still remain divided from their Catholic brothers and sisters.

Within the Protestant world itself, the World Alliance of Reformed Churches and the International Congregational Council united in 1970, reflecting unions between those two confessional bodies in various countries (e.g. India, England and Australia). Three years later the signing of the Leuenberg Agreement and the creation of the Leuenberg Fellowship (now the Community of Protestant Churches in Europe – CPCE) allowed Lutheran, Reformed and United churches in Europe to declare full communion with each other. The rift between Lutheran and Reformed which had opened at Marburg in 1529 was finally bridged.

2 A SPEAKING GOD AND A LISTENING PEOPLE

Reformed Christians are a praying people. As Karl Barth said, 'To be a Christian and to pray are one and the same thing; it is a matter which cannot be left to our caprice. It is a need, a kind of breathing necessity to life.'[1] Indeed, he once argued that the Reformation was one continuous act of prayer.[2] Doing theology, thinking about God and humanity, was for Barth impossible, except as an act of prayer. Historians would justly argue that much in the Reformations of the sixteenth century was very far from an act of prayer. However, at the heart of the movement was a spiritual struggle, a wrestling with the ways of God with men and women, which was intimately connected with the study of Scripture. That worked itself into the personal and public spirituality of the Reformed movement. Spiritual time was reorganised.

The emergence of Reformed worship

The complex pattern of the medieval liturgical calendar was put to one side. The major festivals – Easter, Ascension, Pentecost, Christmas – were still celebrated, but on Sundays. Sunday was a full holiday, Wednesday a partial one. That re-ordering of time was worked out in the continual play of Scripture and prayer throughout the week. Calvin's Geneva was drenched in worship and prayer. The Reformed movement was not a retreat from spirituality, but a bold and radical engagement with the God who spoke through Scripture.

There were four Sunday services. The first, at dawn, was intended for servants and others whose duties would occupy them for the remainder of the day. Its pattern mirrored the main service at eight, so on Sundays when the Lord's Supper was celebrated at eight, it was also celebrated at dawn. The noon service was for children and catechumens. The final preaching service was at three (two in the winter). Calvin normally preached at the eight and the three unless important duties demanded he be elsewhere.

Daily preaching services were held throughout the rest of the week, with Wednesday designated especially as a Day of Prayer. Preaching took the form of *lectio continua*, so there was continual movement through Scripture. The Day of Prayer was a specifically Reformed innovation, with its origins in Strasbourg. The working day did not begin in Geneva until worship was concluded on Wednesdays, and the pattern followed Sunday mornings, with provision for both dawn and eight so that as many as possible could attend. Calvin published a liturgy for it, which focuses on confession and intercession, but thanksgiving for specific mercies could also be included. Calvin loved the Psalms. On the Day of Prayer he focused on psalms of petition, reserving the psalms of thanksgiving for the Lord's Day.[3]

The Reformed always sought (theoretically) for a balance between the Word and the sacraments. Both the reading of Scripture and the administration of the sacraments conveyed the reality of God to his people, so the sermon as well as the Supper demanded epiclesis, or as Calvin's liturgy has it, an 'extempore prayer for illumination-sealing'. Through Scripture, through preaching, God comes.

Preaching

The American church historian Mark Noll notes: 'By the deductive reasoning of some modern intellectuals, as well as to some contemporary Catholics, Lutherans, and high-church Anglicans, Calvinism looks like a thin religion. In point of fact,

the Reformed faith was a great fountain of piety.' The reason
for that piety, and for the power of Calvinism in re-shaping
early modern Europe and North America, was: 'when pious
Calvinists began to ask, How should we live in the world? they
answered by looking to the Bible as a guidebook for life as well
as for its message of salvation.'[4]

The Bible is the heart of Reformed spirituality. It remains
dominant in Reformed worship, despite Calvin's insistence
that Word and sacraments should be held in equilibrium.
Private devotion within the Reformed family centres on the
methodical reading of Scripture. Its theological method is to
use Scripture as the measure of all, subordinating reason and
tradition in a way which is foreign to Catholic and Anglican
theologians. And, as Mark Noll notes, it guides the ways in
which ethics is done and politics is practised.

To be Reformed is to be caught in the dynamics of the Word,
because Scripture is one of God's appointed trysting places,
where the Word spoken before all time, the Word incarnate
and the words written about the Word become, through the
activity of the Spirit, the living Word. A measure of the
Reformed's commitment to the Bible is the extent to which
they disagree about it. Those disagreements are, of course,
largely post-Enlightenment disagreements, consequent on the
questions raised by philosophy about the limits and extent of
knowing, and in particular, how the supernatural might be
known. Reformed theologians and communities differ radi-
cally, but underlying those differences is a shared passion for
the Word.

The Reformed tradition is a broad family, from Ian Paisley
to Walter Brueggemann, from Robert Schuler to John Hick,
from Francis Schaeffer to C. S. Song. They wouldn't agree
about much, but each would give testimony to the centrality
of encountering Scripture in their spiritual and theological
journeys.

Spiritualities are partly formed by disciplines. Regular
worship is a central discipline for all Christians. Reformed
liturgy is, as it were, a series of performances of the biblical

symphony. It is structured around the Word, preparing to hear it, listening to it, entering into its exposition either through listening and thought, or by more active participation and then preparing to live it in the world. Week by week huge intellectual and practical energy is put into that activity. It is a, sometimes 'the', major item of the local congregation's production cycle.

Calvin, whose life centred around preaching, twice on Sundays and on Wednesdays, had an almost sacramental understanding of Scripture and preaching. Here, just as in the Eucharist, the divine was mediated through the human by the power of the Spirit. That is why preaching should be preceded by an epiclesis, or as Calvin called it, a prayer for illumination. Calvin lived long before the Reformed theological world tore itself apart on such questions as the verbal inerrancy of Scripture, which is why proponents of both sides of the argument can mine his works with equal success. Calvin would not even have understood the question. The wonder of Scripture for Calvin was that it was a very human thing and also the vehicle for the very presence of God. Ever the sophisticated humanist stylist, he commented:

> God comes down to *earth* that he might raise us to *heaven*. It is too common a fault that men desire to be taught in an ingenious and clever style ... Hence many hold the Gospel in less estimation because they do not find in it high sounding words to fill our ears ... But it shows an extraordinary degree of wickedness that we yield less reverence to God speaking to us, because he condescends to our ignorance: and therefore when God prattles to us in Scripture in a rough and popular style, let us know that this is done on account of the love He bears us ...[5]

The wonder is that common words, like simple bread and ordinary wine, can become the bearers of the Christ. The preacher is part of that sacramental chain. Calvin's language is extravagant: 'Christ acts by [preachers] in such a manner that He wishes their mouth to be reckoned as his mouth, and their lips as his lips'; 'Christ reigns whenever He subdues the world to Himself by the preaching of the Gospel'; 'Since, therefore, the whole face of the world is disfigured ... there are good grounds for saying that godly teachers renovate the world ...' Preaching is part of the work of salvation, and also part of God's process of renewing creation. Balanced by the Eucharist, preaching is a critical part of the divine economy. The Reformed have held that position with reverent tenacity through the buffeting of nearly half a millennium of intellectual waves.

In 1901 P. T. Forsyth had pronounced preaching 'the sacrament which gives value to all other sacraments',[6] and 40 years later, in one of the great works of Reformed spirituality, *The Servant of the Word*, Herbert Henry Farmer wrote:

> A sermon is not an essay in which you give utterance to your views and impressions of life, though it could hardly fail to contain in some measure your views and impressions of life ... It is not a theological lecture ... It is not a discussion of political and social and international affairs ... It is not instruction in Christian morals ... It is God's great activity of redemption in history in the world of persons ...[7]

Each time the symphony of God's love is played out in Reformed worship, the instruments used include the mouth of the preacher and the ears of the listener (and active listening is far from a passive art). Preachers therefore need their ears attuned to Scripture and the God who speaks through it. Ministerial life has changed somewhat since the great Alexander Whyte was minister of Free St George's in Glasgow at the end of the nineteenth century, but for forty years he jealously guarded four hours a day at his desk – but there again, he was preaching or giving about five addresses a week. His method was constant reading, note-taking and the use of an interleaved Bible. He wrote to his nephew: 'The Bible deserves all our labour and all our fidelity; and we are repaid with usury for all the student-like industry we lay out upon it.'[8]

It is all too easy to dismiss mere words, without realising that words shape everything, even in a visual age.

Walter Brueggemann and a post-modern theology of preaching

It is words that create hatred and violence, words that bring nations to war, words that offer visions of how different things might be, words that let love loose. Language is wonderful, and God became language. So, words, especially those words about God and of God, should be cherished. Post-modern theology and biblical studies readily embrace the power of rhetoric and the world-creating possibilities of language. Walter Brueggemann, the most persuasive Reformed advocate of such approaches to the Bible and preaching, juxtaposes what he calls 'the Enlightenment text' against the liberating, imaginative possibilities of Scripture. If the former encourages an economics of consumerism, relentless growth and 'Euro-American privilege', the latter offers an alternative kingdom, shimmering just beyond the offering of faith. It is 'the voice of free holiness that refuses to let us be where we are on our own terms'.[9] It offers God's alternative world.

His theology of preaching is rooted in his Old Testament scholarship and the primacy which he affords to Israel's praise. God lives in Israel's liturgical practice, and it is therefore her worship that makes God's alternative world available. Christian preaching is a continuation of that witness. The liturgical acts of God's people – doxology, prayer, songs, laments, Scripture (eventually) and sermons – are 're-scriptive'. They can rewrite the everyday text with God's alternative world.

In his 1989 Lyman Beecher lectures on preaching, *Finally Comes the Poet: Daring Speech for Proclamation*, Brueggemann explores the role of the preacher. Three theological and psychological realities are acting on humanity, and therefore on any congregation. The first is sin and guilt. We are a people whose lives have gone wrong. We live out distorted relationships to money and sex,[10] we can't get along with our global neighbours, and sometimes not even with the ones next door, and what we have done to creation is writ large in every broadsheet. And with the sin goes alienation and guilt, and so clever are we that we know very well how to bury all of that, and with Jeremiah cry 'Peace, peace' when there is no peace.

Second, we have a vague nagging feeling inside us that it shouldn't be like this, that there is more to living than being trapped inside this 'self' that I can't get out of. And we are faced with two temptations. The first is to fall into the secular paradigm, that this 'self' is the measure of all, and that there is no reality beyond what it can see and measure. The second is to fall to the opposite, religious pole and perceive the holy and almighty God as the only reality. Either I'm so big that God can't get in, or God is so grand that I can't get an audience, and that reduces me to impotent rage.

Third, we are endlessly restless. We live within a global economic system which is disproportionate, and our anxiety makes us acquisitive. The whole structure of our culture is about getting more. But we do not find rest as we shop; rather, it adds to our restlessness. As the foolish farmer who built bigger barns found, life's meaning is not to be found in acquisition. Indeed, given the inequalities of our economic system, it adds to our guilt and restlessness because we realise that our consumption is exacerbating the poverty of others.

That is who we are. That is the human condition which the preacher addresses. But it is only partly who we are. We are also baptised people, and baptised people have a different identity which subsists in a different nexus of relationships. We are signed. We are part of a covenant. We are God's. We have been bought at a price. From Exodus to Calvary and onwards, Scripture traces that price and that reality. God brings us out of the oppression of sin and alienation into affirmation and life. We are God's, and God's rule will triumph, and the disproportion will end. Babylon will not triumph endlessly.

Teetering on the edge of the kingdom is the Christian condition. We live with one and a half feet in Babylon, and a few toes dipped into the kingdom waters which are ours by baptism. People of faith live on that continuum between the immediacy and the distance of the kingdom. The question which faces the preacher is how the people of faith can be addressed, and sustained, and moved a little further towards the kingdom.

That process of transformation can never be the outcome of coercion. Rather, suggests Brueggemann, borrowing insights from anthropology and sociology, it is woven from the warp of 'cognitive dissonance', that sense that things should be different to the way they are, and the weft of the playful consideration of alternative realities. That is where preaching is situated: 'Preaching is not only the announcement of the alternative but the practice of the very liminality that does not yet know too much.'[11]

It is, however, grounded in baptism, and baptism implies two disciplines: obedience and listening. Baptism is a commitment to God's alternative world, whether symbolised by the joy of immersion or the magically scandalous hope of claiming infants as within the covenant. That is to say, it is a commitment to Christian imagination, to the skills of living subversively in Babylon. It is the liturgical bedrock of all the Gospel proclaiming and doing that constitutes the Church's life. Everything we do arises from baptism.

The implication of baptism is the beginning of a journey of growth into God. That is a growth into the ways of God, and we cannot discern the ways of God for ourselves. The wonder of the human condition is that whilst we were seeking God, God sought us. Abraham did not find God. God found Abraham. Christianity is about being encountered by God in Jesus Christ. The initiative is God's. That is grace. The baptised encounter the revelation of God, firstly (chronologically, if we are infants) through the sacraments, for as Brueggemann so beautifully puts it, '[the] Word has its habitat in Sacrament'.[12] But if firstly through the sacraments, then secondly through the fellowship of those who are our companions in the covenantal baptismal way, the Church, and finally (and most significantly) in the Word which confronts us, engages our imagination and intellect, and mediates Christ to us. It teaches us how to make choices, to do this rather than that, so that we might exchange our restless acquisitiveness for sabbath rest, find that our yearning for something else is sated by communion with the living God, and discover that guilt is assuaged by the balm of weekly, daily, hourly forgiveness. And that is a life-long journey.

Second, Brueggemann argues, we are a people made to listen. Post-Enlightenment people find it hard to listen, for they have been taught that the self is the measure of reality, and that autonomy is a moral imperative. The Judeo-Christian tradition presents an alternative reality – not 'I think therefore I am', but 'I am commanded therefore I am'. It speaks of a people created to be in communion with each other and with God, of a people created to listen to the One who spoke creation into being.

The spirituality of the listener

However (as Calvin noted), it is in being received and heard that the Gospel becomes effective. Reception and translation into changed lives and a renewed society should be expected to follow the proclamation of the Gospel. That is one reason why those who have written systematically about preaching, from Augustine to Buttrick and McClone, have shown an intense interest in those who listen and hear, and the methods by which they listen and hear.[13] The power of the sermon has been remarkable. It was the rhetorical form that allowed New England to develop an identity as a covenantal people dedicated to God's Word and therefore eschewing the authority of

Britain, thus eventually lending defining shape to America's self-understanding.[14]

Bernard Lord Manning, son of an English Congregational minister, and a Cambridge historian, gave an address to ordinands in 1931. It is a rare instance of a sermon listener exploring the responsibilities of listening. He told them:

> We who go into pews ... go because we believe that a pew is somehow different from a seat in a cinema or a lecture room ... You want the theatre and the lecture room to do what they are supposed to do, to act in character, to be true to form: to be a theatre and a lecture room all the time and as hard as they can. So with the preacher. If I go to church I want the preacher to preach, to look as if he was preaching and to talk as if he was preaching ... If the preacher feels that he has to apologize for preaching by behaving as nearly as he can as if he were doing something else he had better give it up.

He listens because he must, for 'in the preached Word Christ Himself is set before us as He is set forth in the Bread and Wine of the holy Supper.'[15]

But if Manning thought the listener had responsibilities, so too did the preacher. 'The study of his flock and the study of divine things: these are the two eyes of the faithful minister of the Word.' Preaching should be interesting, devoid of professional jargon, and pertinent: 'Remember that what is committed to you is the cure of souls, not the instruction of the intellect.' In other words, preaching is a churchly activity. It does not exist in a vacuum but is crafted from pastoral relationships.

For preachers, then, there can be no escape from that continual wrestling with Scripture. And after the wrestling comes the offering, lifting to God this paltry 20 minutes, this inadequate, scratchy performance in the hope that the miracle of grace which unites the preacher's weakness and God's strength will happen once more and God's people will be fed.

The miracle is that it does happen. Alexander Whyte's biographer tells the story of the elder who came to Whyte's vestry after one particularly memorable New Year's Eve sermon. 'It went to my heart as if you had come straight from the Audience-chamber', he said, to which Whyte replied, 'And perhaps I did.'[16] So, at the heart of Reformed spirituality is Scripture, which forms and re-forms us, week by week, day by day. That is the core discipline.

Public prayer

Public prayer surrounded the sacramental reality of the sermon and the Lord's Supper – prayers of confession, for illumination, and of intercession. From its foundation, the Reformed movement never doubted the centrality of public prayer. In the very earliest days of the Reformation – for example, in Strasbourg – traditional Latin prayers were simply translated into the vernacular, albeit with a judicious theological eye for such infelicities as intercessions to the saints. At Strasbourg, public forms of confession, supplication and intercession emerged. The former was scripturally modelled and took printed form in the 1537 *Strasbourg Psalter*, and from there to Calvin's *Genevan Psalter* of 1542, and thence via John Knox into the several generations of the *Book of Common Order* of the Church of Scotland. The latter showed signs (in length at least) of patristic models, which is unsurprising, given the adept patristic scholarship of such Reformers as Bucer and Calvin. This was not unlearned experiment, but a return *ad fontes*, a search for models. If printed liturgical prayers were part of the tradition from the beginning, so too was extempore prayer. In the *Strasbourg Psalters* the two principal prayers are set out liturgically, but stand alongside a clear understanding that other prayers in the service are expected to be either prepared or performed extempore by the minister.[17] Calvin used both forms, normally following the book for confession and intercession, but allowing a beautifully disciplined sense of extemporaneity in his prayers following the sermon, hundreds of which have survived thanks to the skill of the stenographers who recorded his every word. Nonetheless, it is clear that he did not think this gift was given to every minister. It was prayer shaped by the contingency of the sermon, yet crafted from the pastoral heart of the preacher, thus linking Word and world. For example, after a sermon on 1 Corinthians 1:1–5 in October 1555, Calvin prayed:

> that those who are now separated from us may be united [with us] in a true brotherhood; and that God may advance His word more and more, so that it may be a bond to reunite what is now separated throughout the world, and by this means may we all be able to call upon Him with one voice.[18]

Already one begins to see the balance between form and freedom which is one of the axioms of Reformed liturgy and spirituality. Books of prayers and disciplined sets of spiritual exercises are valuable, but never determinative. Equally, freedom can never be absolute; it always requires the discipline of form.

That balance, so clear and striking in the early liturgies, was tilted in the direction of extempore prayer by the hugely influential (in the English-speaking world) Westminster Directory of 1644. A compromise between the Congregational and Presbyterian strands of the tradition, this was a recognition of the importance that the Congregationalists placed on the inspiration of the Spirit, and of the general Puritan distaste of the 'read' prayers of the Book of Common Prayer. Order and form remained a significant need, but the Spirit-led creativity of ministers gained power. The Directory was intended to provide ministers with

> some help and furniture, and yet not so as they become hereby slothful and negligent in stirring up the gifts of Christ in them; but that each by taking heed to himself and the flock of God committed to him, and by wise

observing of divine providence may be careful to furnish his heart and tongue with further or other materials of prayer and exhortation, and shall be needful upon all occasions.

The weakness of the Directory was apparent in the long prayer before the sermon – 'a new fancy of the Independents ... contrair to all the practice of the Church, old or late', grumbled Robert Baillie with some justice. It became a catch-all that included confession, supplication, intercession and praise – often at inordinate length. Confession was particularised and detailed, and intercession was expected to cover the propagation of the Gospel to all nations, the conversion of the Jews, distressed Christians, Reformed churches, the king (for the conversion of the queen), ministers, universities, city and congregation, civil government, those in distress, seasonable weather, and averting God's judgement.[19]

It was a dangerous strategy because it gave responsibility for the prayers of the people into the hands of ministers, who were unequally gifted in the art of extempore prayer. Free prayer under the guidance of the Spirit, which was to become a marked feature of some parts of the Reformed tradition, is widely misunderstood. It was never intended to be unprepared prayer. The great Puritan theologian William Perkins was quite clear that leading the prayers of the people was part of the prophetic task of the minister. If that work were to be done conscientiously, it needed to arise from studied meditation on the subjects concerned in the days leading up to the conduct of worship. Manuals to guide ministers in this art were plentiful. They included the biblical commentator Matthew Henry's *A Method for Prayer*, which went through 30 editions between 1712 and 1865, and the hymn-writer Isaac Watts' *A Guide to Prayer* of 1715. In *A Book of Personal Religion* Nathanial Micklem could claim that this was still the best guide for ministers on this subject. Watts wisely notes that the attainment of the gift of prayer depends on avoiding the extremes of 'confining ourselves entirely to precomposed forms of prayer' and 'an entire dependence on sudden motions and suggestions of thought'.[20] When Murdo Ewan Macdonald was a theological student at St Andrews, he found himself preaching regularly to the congregation at the Martyrs' Church, which included his professor of systematic theology, Donald Baillie. Baillie (one of the great preachers of his day) generously tutored him in preaching, and then turned to his conduct of worship. Macdonald protested that he never wrote his prayers, and Baillie replied, 'That is very obvious. I have listened to you conducting worship at least six times and your prayers are marked by untidiness and repetition.' Then, opening his Bible, he made Macdonald read aloud Psalm 51, and commented, 'That is a prayer of confession. It is in the Bible and it is written.' A similar exercise followed with the prayer of thanksgiving that is Psalm 103. 'There and then', said Macdonald, 'I experienced a Damascus Road liturgical conversion. Ever since that afternoon ... I have meticulously written all my prayers, even more carefully than my sermons.'[21]

The art of written prayers: George MacLeod and John Baillie

Written prayers can be both art and devotion, a union seen most beautifully in English poetry in the work of George Herbert. Whilst his theological indebtedness to Calvinism is clear, his centrist position in the Stuart church meant that his prayers were intensely private rather than public and liturgical. The confluence of the extempore and the written in Reformed liturgy led to a rather different focus. So, private meditation articulates and shapes the prayers of the people as the minister/worship leader seeks to give them voice Sunday by Sunday, and in its turn the written liturgy can inform and shape private devotion.

The prayers of George MacLeod, the founder of the Iona Community, take flight from the launch-pad of creation, in which he expects to meet the cosmic Christ. The material is, for him, the vehicle of the spiritual, and thus sacred. That is reflected in the title of his book of meditations, *The Whole Earth Shall Cry Glory*. They are passionately crafted. As Ron Fergusson notes in his introduction, 'Five hours preparation for a five minute prayer was by no means unusual.'[22] The language is contemporary, idiosyncratic, self-consciously Celtic, vividly particular. The range is wide: a free-flowing, eucharistic prayer for a folk communion ('this bread is vibrant with You, who inhabits all things, and this wine pulsates with You'); a fine four-fold meditation on the invisible Christ always present above, beneath, behind and within us; a passionate cry for peace; and a hymn of delight to the fashioner of Iona's beauty:

> Almighty God, Creator:
> the morning is Yours, rising into fullness.
> The summer is Yours, dipping into autumn.
> The vibrant grasses, the scent of flowers, the lichen on the
>   rocks, the tang of seaweed,
> All are yours.
> Gladly we live in this garden of creation.

But that delight leads to a perception that 'creation is not enough', that decay is embryonically present in beauty, just as 'lambs frolicking careless' foretell slaughter. So the prayer leads us through creation to God, and deeper into God, for creation cannot be understood without redemption:

> ... always in the beauty: the tang of sin, in our
>   consciences.
> The dry lichen of sins long dead, but seared upon our
>   minds.
> In the garden that is each of us, always the thorn.

Yet the wonder of God is that within the economy of his own being, he has made redemptive provision, and

> ... all are Yours as we yield them again to You.
> Not only our lives that You have given are Yours;

but also our sins that You have taken.
Even our livid rebellions and putrid sins:
You have taken them away
and nailed them to the Cross!
Our redemption is enough: and we are free.

The final stanza of the prayer completes the theological circle, asking the Holy Spirit, 'the Enlivener', to fill us with life as part of the new creation which is already breaking upon us.[23]

Written prayer is a stringent discipline. Whilst it demands the discipline of a poet, the end (intelligibility, and articulating the worship of a community of thoroughly different souls) always tempers the means (just as it does in hymn-writing). It is but a short step from praying to lecturing, from adoring God to telling God what to do. As with extempore prayer, Reformed worship continues to walk a thin line between freedom and form. When it gets it right, it can move to heaven's gate in a way that few set liturgies can. When it gets it wrong, it can fall to depths that set liturgies never plumb.

MacLeod's contemporary, John Baillie (1886–1960), was one of the outstanding theologians and ecumenical leaders of the mid twentieth century, his career divided principally between Union Seminary, New York and the University of Edinburgh. A noted liberal, his roots were to be found in the devout Calvinism of the Highlands where his father (also John) was the Free Church minister at Gairloch, Ross-shire. It was a world in which 'The practice of prayer, private, domestic and public, was given a primary place in the daily and weekly round',[24] and that deep, daily piety formed John Baillie as both Christian and theologian. Not that he would have been happy with such a distinction: 'Prayer, after all, is but thinking towards God. And I believe Jesus would have said that all deep and proper thought about our work must be directed towards God and so be of the nature of prayer.'[25] Thus it was that his prayer desk occupied a central place in his study. Here the mind met the mystery of God:

Almighty and eternal God,
Thou art hidden from my sight:
Thou art beyond the understanding of my mind;
Thy thoughts are not as my thoughts:
Thy ways are past finding out.

Yet hast Thou breathed Thy Spirit into my spirit;
Yet hast Thou formed my mind to seek Thee:
Yet hast Thou inclined my heart to love Thee:
Yet hast Thou made me restless for the rest that is in
   Thee:
Yet hast Thou planted within me a hunger and thirst
That make me dissatisfied with all the joys of earth.[26]

Respect and dignity, adoration and assurance, and the simplicity of the truly wise energise this measured, resonant,
repetitive prose. This is church transposed to prayer desk. The
language is drenched in Scripture, alive with a deep sense of
the Christian past (the echoes of Augustine and Francis are
only the most obvious), yet it is intensely Baillie's own. That in
part explains the remarkable and enduring popularity of *A
Diary of Private Prayer*. So too does the form. This is quite
literally a diary of prayers for each morning and evening of the
month. The rhythm is deliberate. In the morning we are
drawn to God in adoration and thanksgiving, contemplating
the new day, offering ourselves as citizens of God's kingdom to
live in the world's kingdoms for his sake. At night we are given
material to reflect on the day just lived, calling to mind
our discipleship in its vulnerable weakness as well as its
strengths, and bringing our world to God in intercession. On
13 out of 31 evenings we are provided with the opportunity to
confess. That is both psychologically acute and theologically judicious. The dangerous Reformed tendency towards
unhealthy introspection and guilt is held firmly in check.
Forgiveness is a solid reality. Baillie helps us see that our lives
are intimately part of the life of God, and God's life is woven
into ours. He helps us understand the way in which private

devotion in the Reformed tradition is both child and parent of public worship.

As Baillie's work amply confirms, if the Reformed understand prayer as a public act, they also know it to be a private responsibility. 'What advantages and opportunities soever you enjoy for social prayer, do not neglect praying in secret: at least once a day constrain the businesses of life, to give you leave to say something to God alone.' So said Isaac Watts.[27] Such sentiments reach back across Reformed history. Question 116 of the Heidelberg Confession (1563), which was to be determinative of German and Dutch Reformed practice, asks, 'Why is prayer necessary for Christians?' The answer is, 'Because prayer is the most important part of the thankfulness which God requires of us. Moreover, God will give His grace and the Holy Spirit only to those who constantly and with heartfelt longing ask Him for these gifts and thank Him for them.'[28] The weighty chapter on prayer in Calvin's *Institutes* (III.xx) provides a gloss on that terse summary.

Calvin on prayer

Prayer, Calvin tells us, is participation in God's generosity in Christ. God's fullness abides in Christ, 'so that we may draw all from it as from an overflowing spring'.[29] Or, changing his metaphor, 'we dig up by prayer the treasures that were pointed out by the Lord's gospel, and which our faith has gazed upon.'[30] Prayer is relational. It is a profound personal sharing so that, 'having disclosed to the Lord the necessity that was pressing upon us, we even rest fully in the thought that none of our ills is hid from him who, we are convinced, has both the will and the power to take the best care of us.'

There are, according to Calvin, four basic rules of prayer. First, 'we [must] be disposed in mind and heart as befits those who enter conversation with God'.[31] The 'splendid and incomparable benefit' of unburdening ourselves to the generous God who 'gently summons' us, should not be undermined by distraction. There should be a quiet, serious

attentiveness about prayer, a resting in the Spirit who takes
our inadequate, untutored longings and desires and trans-
forms them into prayer. Second, prayer should be forged from
a 'burning desire' to obtain the ends prayed for. Polemic is
never far from Calvin's pen, and he cannot resist a passing
dart at those who 'perfunctorily intone prayers after a set
form'[32] as he journeys to the core of his second rule, that
prayer is about the transformation of the one who prays. It is
about the need to be different. If you don't think you are a
sinner, don't pray for forgiveness. Third, the focus of prayer
should be God, not ourselves. Prayer is not an exercise in
competitive holiness, but rather a search for reconciliation
with the God whose nature it is to forgive. Fourth, prayer
should spring from the 'sure hope' that prayer will be
answered.

Once those rules have been patiently elaborated, Calvin
explores the theological dynamics of prayer which are based
in the intercessory role of Christ.[33] Then, after an excursus
on the 'erroneous doctrines of the intercession of saints', he
turns to examine both private and public prayer. Petition and
thanksgiving should be woven together in private prayer, for
prayer is a seeking of God's glory, and every good that comes
to us should redound to his praise. Human life has no
meaning unless it is caught up into the ecology of God's
blessing, so 'we ought constantly to commit ourselves and all
we have to him.'[34] Private prayer is about conforming ourselves to that reality. Private prayer flows into public prayer,
in the gathering of the faithful for worship at times 'indifferent to God but necessary for man's convenience'.[35] The
watchword for public prayer is decorum and orderliness.
Christ has promised to be where two or three are gathered,
provided 'ostentation and chasing after paltry human glory
are banished.'

However, the heart of his teaching on prayer is the Lord's
Prayer. Calvin finds six petitions in the prayer. Luther found
seven, but Calvin treats 'Lead us not into temptation but
deliver us from evil' as one rather than two. The first three

focus on God's glory, the latter three on the human condition. That was to form a pattern for Reformed reflection and meditation on the Lord's Prayer, but it is important to realise that it harks back to the early Fathers, particularly the writings of Tertullian and Cyprian. The Lord's Prayer is God's 'great fruit' of consolation, for it provides us with settled parameters which allow us to 'know we are requesting nothing absurd, nothing strange or unseemly'.[36] Reformed writers on spirituality have returned again and again to the Lord's Prayer. A conversation between three fine interpreters – Calvin, Barth and Olive Wyon – reveals a common core of Reformed spirituality.

The Lord's Prayer

God, wrote Calvin, is 'diffused through all things ... set beyond all place ... lifted beyond all chance of either corruption or change ... embraces and holds together the entire universe' in 'heaven',[37] yet this God is 'our *Father* in heaven'. The opening address of the Lord's Prayer places us in a trinitarian context, for we know of the Fatherhood of God only through the ministry of Christ. Prayer is therefore an expression of God-given intimacy. However, Calvin is acutely aware of the limits of analogous language. Human parenthood derives from a divine model, not the other way round, for God's love is 'greater and more excellent than all our parents' love'.[38] He writes tenderly and beautifully about the old farmer in the parable of the two sons, whom he understands to be an icon of God: 'for he is not only a father, but by far the best and kindest of all fathers, provided we still cast ourselves upon his mercy'.[39] The old farmer was the father of two sons. Similarly, God is *our* Father, not *my* Father or *his* Father. Jesus uses the pronoun with studied deliberation. This is, for Calvin, the prayer of the citizens of the kingdom, and it is to be lived in the city: 'there ought not to be anything separate among us that we are not prepared gladly and wholeheartedly to share with one another, as far as occasion requires.' And he presses his point home in a moment of remarkable global awareness. There is a sense of mutual responsibility in Christ towards 'all men [sic] who dwell on earth. For what God has determined concerning them is beyond our knowing except that it is no less godly than humane to wish and hope the best for them.'[40]

The first three petitions form a discrete whole. God is revealed in his teaching (Scripture) and in the work of creation: 'he has engraved marks of his glory upon a manifold diversity of works and this rightly calls forth praises from every tongue.'[41] It is this proper praise that is rightly God's that constitutes the hallowing of his name. Barth, whose book on prayer moves seamlessly between theological prose and prayer, realises that the implication of 'hallowing' God's name is that God's name is already known:

> Such a presumption is the basis of prayer. Our Father, in heaven, thou hast spoken to us. In thy Son thou hast made thyself Word; thou hast made thyself perceptible and accessible to us in the flesh, in this world ... We are not alone in this world. Thou hast taken a human face, which thou showest to us, and through it we can understand what thou sayest to us. We do not live in a world without God.

Hallowing, for Barth (and in this he follows Luther), must manifest itself in preaching, so that Scripture becomes a daily word from God – not a truth, or a principle, 'but a living person, the great mystery and the great simplicity.'[42] We come, says Olive Wyon, 'to a God who is present ... we are set free from strain: we are not to try to feel God's presence, or to "realize" it; we are here to accept it as a gift; we do not ask Him to "come" to us: He is here.'[43]

God's name, she continues, 'means his manifested character', which is Love. If God's name is to be hallowed, says Calvin, all 'detractions and mockeries' of God's name should be banished. When God's name is properly 'hallowed', the kingdom comes. That in turn demands a proper shaping of human life so that it becomes what God created it to be. The demand of God is absolute, says Wyon. The model response is

Mary's 'Behold the handmaid of the Lord.' Calvin explores the nature of this submission. The 'desires of the flesh' need the correction of the Spirit, and the thoughts of the mind need the Spirit's ordering. To pray 'thy kingdom come' is therefore to enter into a process of personal change and transformation. With the world in turmoil around him, Calvin suggests that this prayer 'ought to draw us back from worldly corruptions, which so separate us from God that his Kingdom does not thrive within us.'[44] It urges us to spiritual discipline, 'mortification of the flesh' and 'bearing the cross'. Grace was not cheap in Geneva.

Barth discovers new depths in this petition, for he explores the eschatological dimension of the phrase in a way that was foreign to the sixteenth century. The kingdom is 'the life and purpose of the world according as they agree with the intentions of the Creator.' It is justice, peace, reconciliation, the accomplishment of God's will. We and all creation long for that liberation. We cannot create it. God gives it. Yet the stupendous truth is that what will be at the end of all ages is present amongst us. Satan has fallen like lightning (Luke 10:18). Breaking into euphoric prayer in the midst of his lecture, Barth exults: 'Thou hast eliminated the fatal danger under the threat of which we were living. Thou, God, hast been the new man who will not die any more ... In Jesus Christ the world has reached its end and its purpose.' To pray 'thy kingdom come' is to celebrate 'this great movement of God in favour of the human race which began with Christmas, with Easter, and with Pentecost ...' It is to pray that the true reality of the world will be revealed. It is also to announce the transitory and temporary nature of the Church, for 'Fortunately in the kingdom of God there will no longer be need of the church, for Jesus Christ will have finished what he began.'[45]

Praying 'thy kingdom come' has, Olive Wyon comments, 'a very practical reference: what is the sphere in which He calls me to work for Him? Is it in my home? In my factory? In my office? In my school?'[46]

The doing of God's will, on earth as in heaven, also lends a prospect of future glory to the present spiritual struggle: 'just as in heaven nothing is done apart from God's good pleasure, and the angels dwell together in all peace and uprightness, the earth will be in like manner subject to such a rule, with all arrogance and wickedness brought to an end.'[47] That future hope, though, is part of the transformative power of the present, a channel for the Spirit to guide us as we 'learn to love the things that please him and to hate those which displease him.' It is a plea that transformation may happen here, now, pitched between the beginning and the consummation, that (as Barth says) God may 'deign to trouble himself with us and with this world'. Yet because we make our prayers in Jesus Christ, we know that God is precisely that God – the God who bothers with us. His will is being done ceaselessly in heaven, and we pray that it may be done on earth, so that

> the chiaroscuro, this mixture of our sacred and ecclesiastical history, this mixture of sanctity and stupidity, of wisdom and vulgarity, which characterises much of our existence – may all this confusion be dispelled ... May this chiaroscuro not last forever; may we cease misunderstanding, thwarting thy intentions ... liberate us from this endless imperfection of our obedience.[48]

This petition is for Wyon the summation of the Lord's Prayer. With typically shrewd insight, she applies this to the individual soul. Human maturity, and true human creativity, come about only when God's will is done, yet deep down we remain afraid of that ultimate identification, lest 'what I want' conflicts with what God wants. '[I]t takes the whole of life and the whole of us' to perform this petition. It is 'the essence of prayer for everyone, beginners and saints.'[49]

The tone and style of the Lord's Prayer changes markedly in the next three petitions. The rest of the prayer is about 'us'. Give, deliver, lead, rather than thy, thy, thy. The language has moved from devotion to demand. This is about us, our needs, this earth. That is as it should be, for as Barth put it with characteristic directness: 'because there is no human-kind without God (atheism is a ridiculous invention), God commands us to pray, God participates in our affairs and in our needs, in our cares and in our distresses, in our expec-tations, in everything'.[50] However, our own affairs, as Olive Wyon notes, 'are comparatively unimportant save as they are part of the love of God and the will of God. They are of value because we are of value to God.'[51]

But who is 'us'? Calvin is clear. 'We' are the Church, the elect. Barth escapes from that strait-jacket. Who is 'us'? 'Us' means those who want to learn to pray with Jesus, who have answered the call to follow. It is the fellowship of those with the 'God-Man'. It is the 'us' of this world, for those who are 'in Christ' are also 'us' with all their human brothers and sisters, and it is the 'us' who know and live 'the misery of the human condition'. Finally, 'us' is the Church, those who know the fallenness of the world and how incapable humans are of extricating themselves from that state. That is to say, the 'us' are those who have prayed the first three petitions of the prayer,[52] or as Wyon prefers, 'those who have a mission here on earth, and all that happens to us is connected with that.'[53]

'Give us this day our daily bread.' Here the kingdom of heaven touches the reality of human economics, for Calvin is clear that 'bread' means 'all things in general that our bodies have need to use under the elements of this world'[54] – food, clothes, and everything which allows us to eat our daily bread in peace, which presumably extends to the political processes of peace creation. This 'bread' can only be the product of a just economic system, for anything 'we acquire through harming another belongs to another.' If we are to receive 'our daily bread', we must open ourselves to the providential love of God, which encompasses all that builds and sustains human comfort. That is not an easy discipline, as Calvin well knows: 'many who venture to entrust the soul to God are still troubled about the flesh, still worry about what they shall eat, what they shall wear, and unless they have on hand abundance of wine, grain and oil, tremble with apprehension.' Yet the discipline of trusting God's providential ordering of the everyday is an essential step on the journey to gaining a proper perspective on this life, for those who learn to trust God's providential care learn to trust him for the greater gifts of 'salvation and eternal life'. It also lends a proper perspective to ownership, wealth creation and industry. 'Daily bread' is God's gift, whether in abundance or scarcity, and it is the duty of Christians to ask 'only as much as is sufficient for our need from day to day, with this assurance: that as our Heavenly Father nourishes us to-day, he will not fail us tomorrow.' What is ours is not ours but God's, and 'he bestows each little portion upon us hour by hour.'

Interestingly, Calvin, the Reformer with the highest eucharistic doctrine of all, passes over the eucharistic overtones of bread. Barth doesn't. In Scripture bread is the sign of God's grace, manna in the wilderness, promise, presence and complete nourishment. Every biblical meal is 'something sacred, for it is the promise of an eternal banquet, of an everlasting feast.' So, this petition joins the realities of earth's economics with the eucharistic transformation. Today's bread and the promise of the bread of heaven are the antidote for anxiety, for they reveal the continuity of God's concern with our affairs, and therefore of a security which is deeper and profounder than the cruel disjunction between life and death. That concern, that relationship is stronger than death. Those who grow into that understanding ground their lives in the sheer generosity of God the giver. Once more theological argument becomes prayer:

> We are a people in the wilderness, and yet we find ourselves surrounded by the splendours and the riches of creation, and by all thy creatures, and by this covenant of grace which thou hast desired to establish between thyself and us. Thou desirest not our death, but our life.[55]

There is abundant bread for all, and those who receive abundantly must abundantly give.

'Forgive us our sins ...' Calvin notes that here 'Christ briefly embraces all that makes for the heavenly life.'[56] The whole theology of atonement, which is such a significant theological reality in Calvin's work, is caught in that brief sentence. The human race is, as Barth concludes, 'insolvent'. Only God can forgive, but that is God's business in Christ. That forgiveness is, once more, a lever of spiritual change and personal transformation, for it lends us the energy to forgive in our turn. That too is a demanding discipline:

> If we retain feelings of hatred in our hearts, if we plot revenge and ponder any occasion to cause harm, and even if we do not try to get back into our enemies' good graces, by every sort of good office deserve well of them, and commend ourselves to them, by this prayer we entreat God not to forgive our sins.

Yet here too is a gift of God, for if we can forgive, then how much more can we have confidence in God's forgiveness. Human forgiveness, according to Barth,

> is a beautiful thing ... Let us not settle down to enjoy the offences done to us; let us not nurse our grudges with pleasure. Rather, let us retain some humour with respect to our offenders. Let us have towards others this small impulse of forgiveness, of freedom.[57]

God's pardon empowers our pardoning. As God forgives us our sins, he raises our eyes to the road ahead: 'We have only to walk on this road which lies open in the direction of the future. By forgiving us thou hast given us the freedom to travel on it.'[58] Wyon, ever the perceptive spiritual director, notes that God requires a spirit of forgiveness from us, for 'Resentment erects a barrier between ourselves and the love of God through which the rays of divine healing cannot penetrate.'[59] She cites the example of Kierkegaard. He found it impossible to believe that God forgave him, until one day during Passion Week in

1848 when he was well over 30. Reflecting on that experience, Kierkegaard commented: 'when one has thus verily experienced what it is to believe in the forgiveness of sins, he has surely become another man ... Eternally he is young.'[60]

'Lead us not into temptation, but deliver us from evil.' Christians, says Calvin, need the Spirit's aid against the 'many and varied' forms of temptation. On the one hand, the good things of life – 'riches, power, honour' – are so sweet that they lure us from God. On the other, the hard things of life – 'poverty, disgrace, contempt, afflictions' – produce a spiral of despondency that brings about our estrangement from God. This petition of the Lord's Prayer pleads that whatever happens to us, we may turn it to good, 'namely that we may not be puffed up in prosperity or yet cast down in adversity.'[61] Calvin is shrewdly aware of temptation's subtlety. He knows that it might be the destructive wiles of evil, or the testing of God, for the Lord 'daily tests his elect'. It is important to be able to distinguish the source, for whereas God's intention is purification, Satan's is predatory. To defeat evil (whether personified as Satan or not) is beyond human capacity. That is God's territory. For Barth, this evil is the *nihil*, 'the infinite menace of the nothingness that is opposed to God himself.' It is the menace of 'ultimate extinction'. God is superior to this 'absolute evil' which is on the 'far left side' of creation, but we are not. This evil is unreal reality, 'the master' wherever God is absent, for there is no other alternative. It is, he says, 'necessary for us to know the Devil exists, but then we must hasten to get away from him.' The Greek words for 'deliver us', says Barth, also mean 'snatch us from the jaws'. Christ has been there, has unmasked the 'sinister wickedness of the enemy'. We have been 'snatched', and therefore it is right that the Lord's Prayer ends, 'Lead us not into temptation', for 'Art thou not God the Liberator? One alone is able to liberate us in a decisive manner. It is thou. We know now that thou art the great liberator ... Thy love is efficacious. It delivers once and for all.'[62]

The closing benediction of the prayer, that God's 'is the

kingdom, the power and the glory', Calvin notes, 'is firm and tranquil repose for our faith.' It is the reason we should pray, for neither kingdom, nor power, nor glory can be 'snatched away' from the Father. That is an appropriate end for a Reformed reflection on the Lord's Prayer. Reformed spirituality is captivated by the glory and the graciousness of God. The wonder of life, for Calvin, for Barth, for Wyon, is that this God has to do with us, that his life is intimately part of ours, and that our living is part of the life of the holy and blessed Trinity. The prayer our Lord gave us is the gateway to that life.

3 A CHOOSING GOD AND A CHOSEN PEOPLE

> Make me a captive Lord,
> and then I shall be free;
> force me to render up my sword,
> and I shall conqueror be ...

wrote the blind Scottish minister, theologian and poet George Matheson in his *Sacred Songs* (1890). This enduringly popular hymn explores the paradox of grace which is at the very heart of Christian discipleship. True selfhood, independence and freedom are to be found not in determined egotism, but in surrender to God. To be God's captive is truly to be free. The hymn continues by exploring how strength is to be found when the Christian is imprisoned within divine arms. The human heart is 'weak and poor' until enslaved by God's 'matchless love'. Human power flickers faintly until God breathes from heaven and his breath energises the human fire. Should my will wish to reach 'a monarch's throne/ it must its crown resign'.

By the time he wrote that hymn, Matheson had survived a crisis of faith that drove him to the verge of atheism. His journey back was provided by a combination of German idealist philosophers and Romantic theologians, in particular Hegel and Schleiermacher. In their work he discovered a way to speak with renewed vitality and passion of the purposes of God revealed in Christ before the foundation of the world, and a catholicity of spirit which enabled him to see that purpose being worked out within the Church and beyond it. In a surviving sermon plan on Revelation 13:8 ('the Lamb slain from the foundation of the world'), he explains:

> Idea is, Christ's death not an accident but part of a system. It also indicates that the system is one of love. Calvary older than Eden, and the plan for redemption precedes the fact of creation ... the work of God in the creation, prefigures sacrifice. All things shine by passing into the life of others: the seed into the flower, the sun into nature, the sea into the reflection of light ... Exhibit then how Christ was 'slain from the foundation of the world.'

He pursued the same theme (and the same text) in a later devotional work, *Leaves for the Quiet Hours*:

> Thou Lamb, slain from the foundation of the world, Thou art the Light thereof! When God said, 'Let us make man!' He meant not Adam but Thee. Thou art the plan of the great building; to Thee all things move.[1]

That sense of purpose, of providential government, of all things coming together 'according to the plan which [God] had formed from all eternity in Christ Jesus our Lord', is at the heart of Reformed spirituality. In *Leaves for the Quiet Hours* Matheson continued, using his own blindness as an exemplar:

> I have seen the artist lose his eyesight and I thought it an unrighteous thing. But if Thy type of sacrifice is the plan of the Architect, I understand. If Thy cross is Creation's crown, I understand. If the Celestial City is a home for hospital training, I understand. If Thine angels are all ministering spirits, I understand. If the purest robe is not the white robe but the robe *washed* white, if the goal of man is not Eden but Gethsemane, if the glory of Thy Father is the sacrificial blood of love, then I have found the golden key, in Thy Light I have seen Light.

Paradox and mystery are part of discipleship's currency. Matheson seeks neither to minimise nor excuse that. However, he finds an ability to cope with both through a reflection on divine sovereignty strikingly understood (in a remarkable anticipation of Barth) as Calvary before Eden. Although one of the first popularisers of German theology in the 1870s, Matheson remained profoundly Reformed. Election, predestination and providential purpose form the backbone of his work – albeit seen through the lens of Schleiermacher.

Questions of election and predestination have ricocheted back and forth throughout the history of Reformed thought. At times the debate has been acrimonious, resulting in punishment and occasionally death. Matheson's crisis of faith shows him to be part of the post-Enlightenment theological world. In that world God's love and what we know of that love in Jesus Christ are amongst the most highly prized theological insights. That separated Matheson from the classical world of Reformed theology which placed supreme importance on God's sovereignty and the working out of God's will. However, his passionate commitment to the primacy of God's purpose – the Lamb slain from before the foundation of the world, and Calvary preceding Eden – forms a bridge to that world.

In that system the logical order of the doctrines of election and salvation mattered hugely. The theological revolutions of the Reformations were partly determined by an Augustinian monk's inward journey. Martin Luther – monk, priest and professor of theology – could not find peace with God. Whatever the cause, he was paralysed by a sense of his own unworthiness, and however earnestly he used devotional disciplines and ascetical practices, he was unable to bridge the gulf between himself and God. His fear of God and his sense of his own sinfulness was so intense that he had to be restrained at the altar whilst celebrating his first Mass, for fear that he would run away. His slow discovery, through the study of Scripture, that God loves us despite our unloveliness, that 'whilst we were yet sinners Christ died for us', was to relocate the relationship between God and humanity. It was to be located not in mediated sacraments, nor in ethics (good works), but in faith. Looking back in 1545 to the discovery of this new understanding, Luther wrote:

> I began to understand that ... the justice of God is revealed through the Gospel, but it is a passive justice, i.e. that by which the merciful God justifies us by faith, as it is written: 'The just person lives by faith.' All at once I felt that I had been born again and entered into paradise itself through open gates.[2]

Once Luther had defined the relationship between God and humanity in this way, it should have been clear that predestination was going to be a problem. If the will is indeed in bondage, if the self is inextricably curled in upon itself by sin, and faith is a gift of God, then the next logical step would seem to be that God decides to whom the gift shall be given. However, Protestant theology only slowly came to terms with this reality, and it was not until the second generation of Reformers that the question came to prominence.

Reformed theology is primarily scriptural theology, but any reading of early Reformed theologians shows them to be diligent students of the early Fathers. The doctrine of predestination is not a Reformed invention. It is to be found in Scripture, and in the Fathers, and above all in Augustine. God, according to Scripture, is a God who calls and chooses. God chooses Abraham to be a great and mighty nation (Gen. 18:19). God summons Moses to go and confront Pharaoh and demand that the Hebrews be set free (Exod. 4). God chooses Israel and makes them an elect nation for no other reason than that he loves them (Deut. 4:37). Poor, trembling, anxious Jeremiah is told, 'before I formed you in the womb I knew you, and before you were born I consecrated you' (Jer. 1:5), and the psalmist admits, 'it was you who formed my inward parts, you knit me together in my mother's womb' (Ps. 139). Jesus calls his disciples with the same peremptory authority, and the Church is described as 'a chosen race, a royal priesthood, a holy nation' (1 Pet. 2:9). In John's Gospel

Jesus says, 'You did not choose me but I chose you' (John 15:16).

If Scripture portrays the relationship between God and humanity as intimate and personal, the free activity of a free and sovereign Being, it is equally insistent that all is encompassed by the knowledge of God. Peter at Pentecost speaks of the crucifixion of Christ as being 'the definite plan and foreknowledge of God' (Acts 2:23). Paul, in one of his densest and finest pieces of theological exposition, writes: 'those whom he foreknew he also predestined to be conformed to the image of his Son' (Rom. 8:29). The letter to the Ephesians describes believers as 'chosen and destined by God the Father and sanctified by the Spirit to be obedient to Jesus Christ' (Eph. 1:5), a theme echoed in 1 Peter, which is addressed to 'the exiles of the dispersion'. In the mystical poetry of the Revelation of John the Divine we are reminded that the inhabitants of the earth are divided into those who have their names written in the Lamb's book of life 'from the foundation of the world' and those who do not (Rev. 17:8).

Any theological system which is to be true to Scripture must take note of the way in which God's purposes are worked out through a series of choices which involve human beings. The paradox of grace, so neatly turned into devotional poetry by Matheson, explores the enduring question of the relationship between God's purposes and the human personality. A call could always be refused. Mary could have said 'No' to Gabriel, just as countless millions through history have said 'No' to the Gospel with varying degrees of politeness. The doctrine of predestination provides an explanation of why Mary said 'Yes', and why others say 'No'. As it does so, it safeguards the sovereignty of God.

The first significant account of predestination comes from Augustine's pen. He sought to explain why some believed and others did not, and arrived at the solution that God gave his grace only to a limited number of people, and passed the rest over. Like Scripture, Augustine is reticent about the fate of the non-elect.[3] On the whole, he speaks of predestination to grace and life, and Aquinas follows him in this. However, later medieval theologians like Isidore of Seville and Gottschalk pursued the argument to its logical conclusion: if some were elected to grace and salvation, the others were automatically elected to damnation. That was the inheritance of the Reformers, and when Luther, Zwingli and Calvin speak of predestination, they are speaking of a double predestination, although all three emphasise the positive rather than the negative aspects of the doctrine.

Predestination, then, is not a Reformed invention, but a theological inevitability. The questions that the doctrine seeks to answer have to be answered. Early Reformed theologians were the inheritors of the way in which the major theologians of the past had handled those questions.

When he was discussing predestination, Calvin knew that he was handling holy mystery, and he argued for a due reserve, protesting against the prying and curiosity which had already turned it into 'a sea of scandals'. The imagery he uses of it – 'abyss', 'labyrinth', 'the deeps of the sea' – is telling.[4] This is a subject to be handled with due deference and humility. He calls it a 'terrible' decree, and finds it dreadful that he has to believe that 'only a small number, out of an incalculable multitude should obtain salvation', but he does not shrink from its logic:

> As God by the effectual working of his call to the elect perfects the salvation to which by his eternal plan he has destined them, so he has his judgements against the reprobate, by which he executes his plan for them. What of those, then, whom he created for dishonour in life and destruction in death, to become instruments of his wrath and examples of his severity? That they may come to their end, he sometimes deprives them of the capacity to hear his word; at other times he blinds and stunts them by the preaching of all.[5]

Calvin places predestination carefully in the *Institutes*. He separates it from the doctrine of God, although it derives from the doctrine of God. It is to be found in Book III, and is part of his treatment of the way in which people receive the grace of God.[6] In other words, he perceives it as a pastoral doctrine, to do with the way in which the work of the Church is received. The focus of Calvin's theology was rather the wondrous majesty of God and his grace displayed to humanity in Christ. Calvin's successors, especially Theodore de Bèze, made predestination more central to their theological concerns. Election and predestination moved to the centre of the theological stage as component parts in the doctrine of God.

A question then arose about the logical ordering of the doctrine. In his cogent and perceptive study, *Election and Predestination*, Paul Jewett offers this analogy in an attempt to help the modern reader appreciate what now appears an arcane debate about theological logic. Imagine a young woman who decides that she is going to buy her fiancé a watch for his birthday. She plans her campaign carefully. She knows what watch she wants, and which shop stocks it. She therefore decides to catch a bus into the nearest town on her next day off, visit the shop and buy the watch. She then does what she has planned. That is the logical order of things. However, temporally she reverses the order. What comes first temporally is the trip to town on her day off, visiting the shop and finally buying the watch.[7]

God, analogously, according to classical Reformed thought, decides what his purpose is – the redemption of the elect – and then plans creation. So, in Matheson's words, Calvary precedes Eden in the purposes of God. That understanding dominates Reformed theology from Calvin to Barth. It is known as 'supralapsarianism' (from the Latin for 'before the Fall'). However, although logically satisfying, it is pregnant with problems. It safeguards God's sovereign will by making God's purpose logically prior to everything else, but that means it cannot avoid the conclusion that God is the author of the sin and the Fall. It is, of course, debatable whether any monotheistic theology can do so, as Second Isaiah boldly realised (Isa. 45:7), but supralapsarianism is peculiarly vulnerable to moral refutation. One Bach does not outweigh ten Belsens.[8] The salvation of the elect cannot justify the horror of sin and evil. That is why a second position emerged early in Reformed thinking about predestination – 'infra-lapsarianism' (from the Latin for 'after the Fall'). Infra-lapsarians argued that after God had created the world, humanity fell, and only then did God decide that the elect should be saved. However, although this position is ethically satisfying – God is remedying sin, not creating it – its logical consequence is that God created a world without first decid-ing what it was for.

De Bèze was a supralapsarian. He therefore avoided the trap that humanity had to fall, but he had to handle the difficulty that he seemed to turn human beings into puppets, and God into a disinterested, if not actually malign, puppet-master.

Predestination was never uncontroversial amongst the Reformed, but the first serious challenge to supralapsarian and scholastic supremacy came from Arminius and the Remonstrants. They argued that God's sovereignty was pre-determined by his justice. God did not arbitrarily condemn unbelievers to perdition. Rather, God foreknew a believer's acceptance of Christ and subsequent perseverance. That foreknowledge preceded election. The orthodox regarded this as making God's grace depend on human decision, and article VII of the Synod of Dort restated the orthodox position clearly:

> Election is the unchangeable purpose of God, whereby, before the foundation of the world, he hath, out of mere grace according to the sovereign pleasure of his own will, chosen, from the whole human race, which had fallen through their own fault, from their primitive state of rectitude, into sin and destruction, a certain number of persons to redemption in Christ, whom he from eternity appointed Mediator and head of the elect and the foun-dation of salvation.[9]

The Westminster Confession is short and blunt by comparison as it restates what was the almost universal understanding of Western Christendom: 'By the decree of God, for the manifestation of his glory, some men and angels are predestined unto everlasting life, and others foreordained to everlasting death.'[10]

The debate about predestination was an intra-Reformed debate. The doctrine was a matter of anxiety amongst Reformed theologians from the earliest days of the movement. Heinrich Bullinger had held out for a more universal understanding of the reach of the Gospel in his *Decades*, and nearly 20 years after Dort, the French Reformed theologian, Moise Amyraut, propounded his own moderate position in his *Brief Traitté de la Predestination* (1634). However, orthodoxy prevailed, and the majority of Reformed confessions (e.g. the Gallican and Belgic) maintain an infralapsarian stance, although some major Reformed thinkers subscribed to supralapsarian positions.

To modern readers these debates can seem arcane and absurd. We 'do' theology and spirituality very differently, preferring to interpret God's sovereignty through the metaphor of God's love rather than his will. Thanks to Barth, we also understand election christologically. Very few modern confessions refer to predestination and most modern Reformed theologians would pay due heed to Barth's critique that the classical doctrine was too speculative, exceeded its biblical warrant and was not sufficiently focused on Christ.[11]

The prominence of predestination in the Reformed tradition was a consequence of Calvin's understanding of the sovereignty of God. Calvin was captivated by the reality and power of God the Creator. This was the God with whom men and women have to do in every moment of their lives – the sovereign, reigning God. Whereas Aquinas understood the aim of being human to be the attainment of the vision of God in all God's perfection, Calvin considered it to be the glorification of God. The 'chief end of man' (*sic*) is, in the words of the Westminster Shorter Catechism, 'to glorify God and enjoy him forever'. Although contemplation and glorification are intimately related, contemplation is essentially passive, whereas glorification is essentially active. They offer different spiritual routes, one drawing the believer ever closer to prayer and adoration, the other inviting active discipleship and a discovery of God in the everyday.[12]

Reformed spirituality emphasises both God's glory and God's purposes in the world. God chooses and elects in Scripture not for whim or fancy, but so that his purposes can be worked out in human history. Election is about purpose and therefore service, participation in the mission of God. It is not something that is deserved, a reward for zealous effort or spiritual striving. John Bell expresses that nicely in his hymn 'We rejoice to be God's chosen':

> We rejoice to be God's chosen,
> not through virtue, work or skill,
> but because God's love is generous,
> unconformed to human will.
> And because God's love is restless
> like the surging of the sea,
> we are pulled by heaven's dynamic
> to become, not just to be.[13]

The positive contribution of the doctrine of election to Reformed spirituality was a sense of liberation, and a sense of calling to live a godly life for the sake of Christ's kingdom. Election could liberate the believer from anxiety about salvation. Indeed, it suggested that placing salvation at the centre of the theological agenda was itself an error, for it allows the self to usurp the place of God. What mattered was the purpose of God, which embraced the whole creation. The joy lay in the perception that God is involved with the world, calling particular groups and people to bring about his salvation. As Colin Gunton noted, God's merciful care for the world 'takes concrete form in election, especially the election of those we might least expect'.[14] Those who are chosen, from the Patriarchs, through the nation of Israel (Deut 7:7) to the disciples and the Church, are not chosen for their own goodness or ability, but because they were in a mysterious way those who did God's will. Election was therefore a liberation from spiritual striving, and it is one reason why historically the Reformed have been wary of spiritual disciplines and exercises. There is a divine objectivity about election which obviates the need for cultivating the soul.

If election can help shape spirituality positively, it can also be (and has often been) dangerous and destructive. It has been blamed for (*inter alia*) the growth of capitalism, the Protestant work ethic, racism and apartheid. Such critiques, especially when they are from such able critics as Troeltsch, cannot be lightly dismissed. There is no doubt that the Reformed tradition has been misused and misinterpreted. Calvin's instinctive wariness about the doctrines of election and predestination led him to separate them from the doctrine of providence in the final edition of the *Institutes*. Previously he had treated them together. He was reaching towards an understanding that whilst election and predestination primarily relate to individuals, providence is rather about God's purposes for creation. So, in the 1559 edition providence becomes part of the doctrine of creation (Book I) and predestination is to be found within his teaching about the Spirit and the Christian life (Book III). Election was, in Calvin's eyes, a doctrine which comforted the believer with the assurance of salvation, the result of unmerited grace. He never intended it to become the lens through which the purposes of creation could be read.

That it became so for a long period in Reformed history was the result of de Bèze's supralapsarianism. Thanks to his inversion of Calvin's doctrinal order, predestination and providence orbited too closely together, and election to salvation became inextricably muddled with the providential movement of history, and the elect nation replaced the elect Church. That was a mistake Calvin would never have made. He would never have confused a group, nation or race with the Church, the elect of God.[15]

Others were more easily confused. In 1640 a New England Assembly passed the following resolution:

1. The earth is the Lord's and the fullness thereof. Voted.
2. The Lord may give the earth or any part of it to his chosen people. Voted.
3. We are his chosen people. Voted.[16]

When Isaac Watts published his translations of the Psalms in 1719, he gave not a second thought to translating 'Israel' as 'Great Britain'. The Preamble to the 1961 Constitution of the Republic of South Africa tells how God 'gathered our forebears together from many lands and ... gave them this their own'.[17] In each of these cases election and a sense of special providence fused, and the legacy was a misdirected understanding of Reformed doctrine which has contributed to the politics of the displacement of native peoples, and the evils of racism and apartheid. It was, regrettably, politically and economically potent.

Election was meant to be a doctrine of assurance, built on the objectivity of God's choice. Salvation was a gift, not a goal to be achieved. What mattered was living the Christian life, holy living that glorified God. Searching the soul for evidence of salvation was an unwanted exercise in self-aggrandisement. Calvin was a fine theologian of the Spirit. The Spirit's role is central in the interpretation of the Word, for it is the Spirit who holds together the Word spoken before creation, the Word made flesh in Christ and the Word made almost sacramentally present in the act of preaching. Similarly, Calvin's eucharistic theology depends on the Spirit making the heavenly Christ food and drink for his earthly people. The work of the Spirit is a significant component in his theology of salvation. Historically, the experiential was be a minor theme in the Reformed symphony, yet it was to gain prominence in the writings of the English Puritans, most particularly in William Perkins, William Ames and Richard Baxter, and in the great American theologian, Jonathan Edwards.

'Puritan', like 'Christian', was initially an insult for those who sought to live a 'pure' life according to Scripture, and in doing so distanced themselves from the accepted conventions of church and state. Puritanism was a significant stratum in English religious life, from the agitation for a church more fully reformed than the Elizabethan church settlement allowed in the 1570s, until the final settlement of England's wars of religion in 1662, when the Act of Uniformity and the Clarendon Code institutionalised religious pluralism and turned many Puritans into nonconformists.

Puritans are easy to identify yet hard to define. They do not subscribe to one ecclesiology, nor one creed, although most (but not all) were committed Calvinists. They are ordained and lay. They are to be found within the established church, yet also outside it. Their theologies and spiritualities are subtly (and sometimes unsubtly) different. Yet they are united by a common seriousness, a commitment to the pilgrimage of holy living in the world rather than apart from it.

The Reformation could be summarised as the rediscovery of the Word. The Word and preaching were at the heart of the Protestant revolution, yet what made Scripture the Word was the Spirit, inspiring the writer and enlightening the mind of the hearer through the work of the preacher. As Richard Sibbes put it, 'the breath of the Spirit in us is suitable to the Spirit's breathing in the Scriptures; the same Spirit doth not breathe contrary motions', and in a memorable medical analogy, 'as the spirits in the arteries quicken the blood in the veins, so the Spirit of God does along with the word, and makes it work.'[18] Calvin would not have demurred, but he would have been decidedly anxious as the Puritan tradition widened and broadened to ask whether the Spirit might act independently of the Word, and at its radical edge formulated the Quaker conception of the Inner Light. However, most Puritans maintained a studied balance in their exploration of the Spirit and the Word. Nonetheless, the development of a theology of the Spirit necessitated an understanding of sanctification. John Owen, arguably the greatest of Puritan

systematicians, Dean of Christ Church and Vice Chancellor
of Oxford University during the Commonwealth, was insistent that the Spirit's work is both objective (it is the Spirit
who communicates the life of the risen Christ to the believer)
and a subjective experience for every Christian. It is 'the
infusion of a new, real spiritual principle into the soul and its
faculties, of spiritual life, light, holiness and righteousness',
which in its turn triumphs over the habitual inclination to
sin.[19] In other words, the evidence of salvation lies in
experience, and experience can be analysed and recounted.
Conversion accounts and spiritual diaries began to be produced, from which it was but a short literary step to the
autobiography. Ironically, the doctrine of election, intended
by Calvin as a spiritual comfort, became a generator of
anxiety. The question of election, of one's eternal destiny,
allowed the self and salvation to slip back to the centre of the
theological agenda. Uncertainty about this critical concern
could be countered by self-examination, by study of the conscience. All leading Puritan writers from Perkins in the
1590s to Baxter in the 1650s lent their weight to this. An
important text was 2 Corinthians 13:5: 'Examine yourselves
to see whether you are living in the faith. Test yourselves. Do
you not realise that Jesus Christ is in you? – unless, indeed,
you fail to meet the test.'

Richard Baxter, ever a wise spiritual guide, accepted that
determination of one's spiritual state was a duty, but he was
very hesitant about the methods that should be employed.
Looking back over his own Christian life, he knew that his
salvation had not evidenced itself in emotion and feeling, and
unlike more prescriptive counsellors, he judged that 'God
breaketh not all Mens hearts alike'. What he looked for was
the result of conversion – a sincere willingness to serve God,
an aptitude to prefer the glory of God to the comforts of the
earth.[20]

Such an aptitude could signify 'a saint', one of God's chosen
ones. Their number, of course, was known only to God, yet
those called to walk in God's way needed the mutual

encouragement of fellowship. Puritan spirituality has an in-built tendency towards separatism. In the generation after the Restoration one poet – Isaac Watts – articulated that exquisitely:

> We are a Garden wall'd around,
> Chosen and made peculiar Ground;
> A little Spot inclos'd by Grace
> Out of the World's wide Wilderness.

Planted by God, watered by the springs of Zion, that the 'young Plantation' may grow, and its perfume and spices of love and joy and faith may be blown by the Spirit, that the Lord may delight in our 'sweet perfumes'. What is striking is the way Watts deliberately and delightedly allows his poem to dip allusively in and out of the eroticism of the Song of Songs (4:12–16). This is election as relationship, and eucharistic fellowship that borrows from George Herbert's 'Love III':

> Eat of the Tree of Life, my Friends,
> The Blessings that my Father sends;
> Your Taste shall all my Dainties prove,
> And drink abundance of my Love.

And the work of the 'elect' Church is to frequent Christ's board:

> And sing the Bounties of our Lord:
> But the rich Food on which we live
> Demands more Praise than Tongues can give.[21]

Watts' singing the bounties of God gave rise to Reformed art of the highest order. In classical Reformed thought, election is a celebration of the purposes of God, a delight in the love and mercy that received supreme expression in the cross of Christ. In his greatest hymn, 'When I survey the wondrous cross', Watts returns the purposes of God to the centre of the theological agenda, at the same time achieving a poised, poetic balance between those purposes and the value of the self which had for so long evaded Reformed theologians.[22]

This hymn is also poetry of the highest order, for the discipline of the hymn is integral to the art. It begins with an air of almost Olympian calm – 'When I survey ...' The word 'survey' suggests detachment, calm, security, seeing the completed whole. It is precisely because of that that Watts can see the cross as 'wondrous' rather than horrific. Yet it is wondrous because it is horrific, a throne because it was an instrument of death. The perspective is formed by Easter, and Watts makes the singer move effortlessly between event and interpretation.

That invitation to multiple readings of the cross is the wellspring of the hymn's emotional energy. Under its force the confident, secure self of the opening lines begins to disintegrate, to be replaced by another self, and the new Adam in Christ displaces the old, egotistic self:

> my richest gain I count but loss,
> and pour contempt on all my pride ...

This is the dynamic of tragedy in controlled miniature – the fall of the original self which leads to true self-knowledge. It is the pattern that we see in Lear and Oedipus. In the first verse sufficiency – 'When I survey ...' – begins a pilgrimage to surrender which ends in the final line of the hymn as the true self emerges – cleansed, purified, arriving at the beginning and knowing the place for the first time, as T. S. Eliot was to put it.

The tragic descent which begins in the last two lines of the first verse is elaborated in the second, and by the third verse the 'I' who began the poem in Olympian detachment is to be found standing at the foot of the cross:

> See from his head, his hands, his feet,
> sorrow and love flow mingled down ...

The imperative 'See' is commanding, unavoidable; the relational involvement of the insistent repetition of 'his' is redolent with pathos. How different, how much less effective would it have been if Watts had written, 'See from his head and hands and feet'. It is the Prince of glory whose life-blood is ebbing, sorrow and love mingling, trickling over the battered body. It is a brilliant image, enabling Watts to hold together the two perspectives of Good Friday and Easter Sunday – the sorrow and misery of the heart of darkness, humanity killing God, and the triumphant realisation that divine love encompasses even that depth of treachery, turning it into the fabric of redemption.

Then comes a vivid splash of colour:

> His dying crimson, like a robe,
> spreads o'er his body on the tree ...

The colour is startling, yet the imagery draws us back, distances us from the reality to which he exposed us in the repetition of 'his'. Crimson, robe, tree – not blood, nudity, cross. It is as if the reader/singer is invited to make that translation, indeed must do so, because that is the route to realisation that the price of redemption was the death of God on Good Friday. And only when we have made the connection, felt it in our hearts, can we respond and complete the tragic cycle by discovering that we will never be our true selves until we give ourselves to the God who died for us:

> then am I dead to all the globe
> and all the globe is dead to me ...

As I sing/read I move from Christ's death to mine, from the world seen from the outside, a globe suspended in space, to the life of discipleship within it:

> Were the whole realm of nature mine,
> that were a present far too small ...

And then he brings the poem to a conclusion:

> love so amazing, so divine,
> demands my life, my soul, my all.

My all – totality – there is no more. The magnitude of God's love is captured in the inevitability of the human response. In the face of such love, nothing less than 'my all' will suffice.

This is a remarkable meditation on the dynamics of the relationship between God and humanity, revolving around the still point of the cross. It is not emotional, dramatic or Baroque, indeed it breathes the controlled rationalism of the classical Reformed tradition. Yet it infuses that rationality with deep devotional passion. Here is the self properly ordered, seen in perspective, understood in the light of the divine purpose. This is a proper spirituality of election.

4 A HOLY GOD AND A WORLDLY PEOPLE

The Reformed and the second commandment

> Then God spoke all these words: I am the Lord your God, who brought you out of the land of Egypt, out of the house of slavery; you shall have no other gods before me. [b] You shall not make for yourself an idol, whether in the form of anything that is in heaven above, or that is on the earth beneath, or that is in the water under the earth. You shall not bow down to them or worship them; for I the Lord your God am a jealous God, punishing children for the iniquity of their parents, to the third and fourth generations of those who reject me, but showing steadfast love to the thousandth generation of those who love me and keep my commandments.
>
> (Exod. 20:1–6 NRSV)

For Augustine, the Western Latin church, and then the Roman Catholic and Lutheran churches, this was one commandment, the first. But for Judaism, the Eastern Orthodox, the Reformed and the Anglican Communion, this was two commandments, the break coming at [b].[1] The fact that there were two systems of numbering the ten commandments had long been forgotten in the Western Church until, in September 1523, Leo Judt, a colleague of Zwingli's in Zurich and a learned Hebraist, stumbled upon it anew, and drew attention to it in a sermon. Not only did the Bible forbid the creation of images, but under this system, it allocated the ban its own com-

mandment. This was not an addendum to the first commandment, but a separate one, and that gave added importance to
its instruction.

Although Judt was not quick to publish his 'discovery', it
took on a life of its own in the pulpit, and was one of the factors
behind the outburst of iconoclasm in Zurich in 1523 following
the Public Disputation. The Strasbourg Reformer Martin
Bucer played a critical role in disseminating this new understanding. First, he incorporated it into the Tetrapolitan Confession, the hastily prepared statement of the four 'Reformed'
imperial cities of Strasbourg, Constance, Memmingen and
Lindau, which was presented to Charles V as an alternative to
Melanchthon's Lutheran Augsburg Confession at the Diet of
Augsburg in 1530. Second, his *Treatise on Images* (1535)
explores the intent of the second commandment in more depth.
Third, he was the mediator of the 'new' understanding both to
Calvin, who spent 1538–41 in Strasbourg, and to Cranmer,
to whom Bucer was both friend and mentor (and if to Cranmer,
then to the Book of Common Payer and Anglicanism).

In a sense Judt's discovery was part of the Reformed
movement's restorationist quest for the unsullied Church of
the New Testament. Calvin believed (wrongly, as we now
know) that there had been no art or images in Christian
churches during the first five centuries[2], and he sought to
return worship to that pristine state. This was far from an
unthinking philistinism. Calvin's theology can best be
understood as a series of fugues on the transcendence of God.
God is God. God is completely other. God is not to be confused with creation. That was the great mistake of the
medieval Church in the minds of all the Reformers. It had
tamed God, made him immanent, confused him with the
bones of saints, holy wells, and sacred objects. The mistake
was so fundamental that an entirely new way of understanding the world was needed, and it was this that Calvin
set out to provide, developing this understanding through the
successive editions of his *Institutes*. He was creating a new
way of reading reality.

There are two sources for a proper understanding of the world – knowledge of God, and knowledge of ourselves. By knowledge of ourselves Calvin also means knowledge of the world and creation, because he understands the individual as a microcosm of creation. God is the source of both these streams of knowledge: 'it is certain that man never achieves a clear knowledge of himself unless he has first looked upon God's face, and then descends from contemplating him to scrutinise himself.'[3] Knowledge of God is both planted in the human mind and written into the structure of creation. It is, in Calvin's thought, there to be accessed. It is objective, out there, available. The problem is not that the creation is ambiguous or obscure, but that the human mind is blinded. Rather than see what is there, human beings prefer their own speculations, fashioning God after their own predilections: 'They do not therefore apprehend God as he offers himself, but image him in their presumption ... they are worshipping not God but a figment and dream of their own heart'.[4] Fallen humanity has become 'a perpetual factory of idols',[5] and imagination forms the production line.

Calvin offered an alternative. Like most medieval theologians, he believed that once the human mind had been 'repaired', it was quite capable of understanding the world as it actually is. The *Institutes* set out the method. First, the proper understanding of God is to be found in Scripture, discerned under the guidance of the Holy Spirit. So, reading Scripture and listening to preaching is methodologically central. Second, Christ forms the bridge between God and humanity. Third, acceptance of Christ through grace brings about a re-creation of the individual and the possibility of living as human beings were meant to live, in a world which Calvin calls the 'theatre of God's glory'. Fourth, God has appointed trysting places – the preaching of the Gospel, and the Lord's Supper – where the benefits of Christ's work can touch the human heart. Hence the importance of the Church.

This, Calvin believed, was the only methodology which would allow human beings to understand themselves and their world properly, and it lies behind the ways in which the Reformed tradition developed. Whereas the pathway of the Lutheran tradition was determined by Luther opposing Law and Gospel, the Reformed traditions were united by the way in which they opposed the visible and the invisible. The transcendent, holy and 'other' God belonged to the invisible and inward universe of faith, and would always elude the skills of traders in the visible. God is

> Immortal, invisible, God only wise,
> in light inaccessible hid from our eyes ...

as the Free Church of Scotland hymn-writer and poet William Chalmers Smith (1824–1908) memorably expressed it.

However, God witnesses to himself, according to Calvin, through the works of nature, and with compelling clarity in Scripture. And therefore the visual and the beautiful have a serious place within the Reformed tradition: 'this skillful ordering of the universe is for us a sort of mirror in which we can contemplate God who is otherwise invisible'.[6] Calvin was caught up in wonder as he contemplated both the intricacy of the human body and the glories of creation: 'astronomy, medicine, the natural sciences ... the liberal arts' are all ways of entering more deeply into 'the secrets of the divine wisdom', and even without their aid, the eye perceives 'the excellence of divine art, for it reveals itself in this innumerable and yet distinct and well-ordered variety of the heavenly host.'[7] The plastic arts in particular are part of this glorious panoply. Sculpture and painting, he assures his readers, are 'gifts of God', but they must be used as God wishes them to be used. The commandments make it quite clear that God cannot and should not be visibly represented, so that 'cannot be done without defacing his glory'. The work of the artist is therefore to sculpt or paint 'that which the eyes are capable of seeing'.[8]

Aniconic spiritual traditions are rarely artistically impoverished – a glance at the exquisite world of Islamic art shows that immediately. Yet in the popular mind, Reformed

Christianity is still frequently perceived as Philistine. The shadow of the image-smasher is long. However, that shadow is also a distortion. Recent studies have begun to provide a more balanced perspective.

A 'worldly' spirituality

Plainness is the opposite not of the visual, but of decoration. The simplicity of early Reformed worship was commandingly visual – plain walls, a simple table, bread and wine, the congregation, and a minister in a black academic gown. It was an emphatic statement which was meant to be arresting, shocking even, in comparison with what it was replacing. The visual statement told the story, namely that the connection between heaven and earth was God in Christ and the Scriptures that bore witness to that. All other symbolic connections had been severed, because they did not work. The visual is inescapable.

Yet it can also be harnessed and used. There is an unexpected yet interesting continuity of the devotional and instructional use of the woodcut across the boundaries of the Reformations. Eamon Duffy has shown how the imagery of the medieval Book of Hours survived the Henrician Reformation and ended up incorporated into Protestant devotion in (for example) *The Booke of Christian Prayers* (1578), framing a prayer by John Foxe which denounces the Pope and celebrates the Marian martyrs.[9] A similar story emerges in Zurich. As early as 1526 Zwingli used simple woodcuts to explore the new Reformed liturgical reality through images. The title page of his *On the Lord's Supper* (a vernacular work intended to be read by the faithful at home) uses four woodcuts of the Passover meal, the collection of manna, the feeding of the five thousand and the Lord's Supper to offer a visual commentary on the meaning and resonance of the new service.[10] The visual has not been abolished, it has been transposed, in this case from the sanctuary to the home.

Calvin swung the devotional pendulum from the Church to the world. God's glory was to be discovered in the world;

the world was the 'theatre' of God's glory. God is, of course, transcendent, beyond the world, and not to be confused with it. Yet the world speaks profoundly of God. For those with eyes to see, who perceive reality through the 'spectacles' of Scripture[11] and the sound knowledge of Calvin's methodology, it is full of 'skillful ordering' and is a rational place. Calvin of course believed that God could intervene, but he also believed that the age of miracles had ceased with the apostles.[12] The sheer otherness of God means that no space is sacred, for God is the elusive absence in the midst of all that is sacred. Or, to put it more positively, all space is sacred because the world crackles with the rationality of God's providential ordering. This is profoundly important for Reformed spirituality. It is in this sense a 'worldly' spirituality. The import of that emerged slowly, both intellectually and socially.[13]

'Mapping' the world

Intellectually Calvin handed on a legacy which included an understanding of the world as a rational place. This understanding, which he had laid down in the *Institutes*, could be summarised, first in words, but after the 1580s, with diagrams and charts (which can be seen as a variation of the visual image). This was partly due to the influence of the French Huguenot logician Peter Ramus (1515–72). Ramus thought that logic was the natural extension of Calvin's way of understanding the world as rationally ordered by God. His work was profoundly influential between 1550 and 1650. What matters now is not his formal understanding of logic (which has not found favour with later logicians) but the way that he sought to organise knowledge. He mapped human knowledge differently, placing things carefully in relation to each other. That 'placing' was significant. A place has a visual component, especially when related to other 'places', and Ramus used diagrams and charts for this 'mapping'. What emerges here is a new way of looking at and ordering the world, a small step towards the inductive method that was to mark the rise of the scientific understanding of the world. The methodology spread quickly. Ramist charts began to appear in Bibles as early as 1586 and diagrams soon became an accepted part of Reformed systematics.[14] The price paid for this re-emergence of the visual was the triumph of logic over Scripture as the organising principle of Reformed thought.

But for all that, it opened up a new way of perceiving and imagining the world. And that was as much about the workings of the mind as the artistic hand. A second, and closely allied development around the 1580s was the emergence in the English Puritan part of the Reformed tradition of what Dyrness terms 'inner picturing'. Musing on the power of the preached Word, William Perkins (1558–1602) noted: 'the sound comes to the eare; and at the same instance the thing signified comes to the mind; and thus by relation the world and the thing spoken of, are both present together.'[15] Reformed Christians were encouraged to paint in their minds those pictures which were denied them on the walls of their churches.

'Inner picturing'

This 'inner picturing' in its turn shaped the rhetoric of preachers and the work of biblical commentators. Matthew Henry's (1662–1714) potently imaginative, visual exploration of the return of the prodigal son shows how moving and powerful it could be:

> How lively are the images presented here! ... Here were *eyes of mercy*, and those eyes quick-sighted: *When he was yet a great way off his father saw him*, before any other of the family were aware of him, as if from the top of some high tower he had been looking that way which his son was gone, with such a thought as this, 'O that I could see yonder wretched son of mine coming home!' This intimates God's desire of the conversion of sinners, and his readiness to meet them that are coming towards him ...

Here were *feet of mercy*, and those feet quick-paced: *He ran*. This denotes how swift God is to show mercy. The prodigal son came slowly, under a burden of shame and fear; but the tender father ran to meet him with his encouragements. [4.] Here were *arms of mercy*, and those arms stretched out to embrace him: *He fell on his neck*. Though guilty and deserving to be beaten, though dirty and newly come from feeding swine, so that any one who had not the strongest and tenderest compassions of a father would have loathed to touch him, yet he thus takes him in his arms, and lays him in his bosom. Thus dear are true penitents to God, thus welcome to the Lord Jesus.[16]

Such an understanding of the ways in which God comes to the individual through the reading and study of Scripture and through the 'sacrament' of preaching is a close cousin of Ignatian spirituality. Both depend on an imaginative engagement with Scripture, with 'picturing'. But there is a significant difference. The Ignatian *Exercises* invite readers to imagine themselves within the biblical stories. Reformed spirituality, with its grounding in the sovereignty and providential love of God, invites believers to see themselves as players in the 'theatre of God's glory', to allow God's story to continue in them. The art historian Erwin Panofsky made a distinction between Ignatian 'ecstasy' and Protestant 'absorption'.[17] It is a distinction which should not be over-played, for the Jesuits have been and are far from politically and socially disengaged, and the Reformed have nurtured their own traditions of prayer. Nonetheless, it provides an important insight into the workings of Reformed spirituality. It is world-focused, and therefore social and political.

Liturgical space

The breaking down of the barrier between the sacred and the secular was one of the profoundest results of the Reformation. The world is God's, and it is therefore all sacred space. It was

Calvin's initial instinct to lock the doors of St Peter's, Geneva outside service hours, lest people should be tempted to go into church and pray, for they could and should pray everywhere. That was a powerful symbolic gesture, albeit one that lacked pastoral tact. In countries where the Reformed Church became the State Church, parish churches remained at the heart of the community, but in states where the Reformed were a minority, new and thoughtful forms of church architecture emerged, fashioned to the expression of a different spirituality.

This can be seen clearly in the emergence of Huguenot temples. Architecture reflected ecclesiology, theology and a restorationist impulse, hence the name 'temple'. The 'church' was the believing community; the building where they gathered was the 'temple'. The divisions of space which were characteristic of medieval churches were abandoned. Cruci-form design and altars gave way to polygonal and basilican forms with the pulpit prominent, because the Reformed believed (as did all the Reformers) that the earliest churches were round and that the clergy presided from the middle so that all could see and hear.[18] Worship was a participative, congregational affair. It was therefore important that the congregation should be able to see and hear, and thus share, in the corporate experience. A nineteenth-century English Congregational minister put it bluntly:

> A dimly lighted Church may do very well for a dark reli-gion or a twilight faith, but never for the intelligence, freedom and confidence of Congregationalism. For my part I care very little what sort of place I preach in, if I have two requisites, light and air, and can see the people well grouped together, not split up into sections by transepts or peeping out of cornices and burrows beneath the roof.[19]

Reformed architecture was liturgically functional. At their best, Huguenot temples (like Salomon de Brosse's 1623 second temple at Charenton) were elegant and simple. They were for congregations, so they had pews and galleries (Charenton had two tiers). But the visual experience did not stop there. There were Decalogue boards, Scripture texts on the walls and silver communion-ware. Aniconic undoubtedly, but also profoundly visual.

Further east, in the Hungarian Reformed Church, the stress was on adaptation rather than innovation. Walls were whitewashed, but folk art flourished. There were beautiful patterns of leaves on the walls (as at Csaroda), magnificently carved pulpits and sounding-boards (as at Takos) and extraordinary painted ceilings (as at Tancs) whose subjects included flowers, snakes, storks, Jonah, a peacock and a pelican feeding its young. This was a strictly regional phenomenon, but an important one, for it shows how subtle and unpredictable the relationship between Calvinism and culture can be in the shaping of the Reformed tradition.[20]

Two examples from the English nonconformist tradition illustrate that further. The first is Union Chapel, Islington, designed by James Cubitt in 1876–79. Cubitt drew his inspiration from the eleventh-century octagonal Santa Fosca in Torcello in Venice. It was a building which inspired Ruskin almost to rapture in *The Stones of Venice*. Clyde Binfield argues that Cubitt deliberately transposed four aspects of the Torcello building into Union Chapel. The first was 'luminousness', the sheer quality of light. The second was the centrality of the pulpit – simple, plain and in the centre of the apse. Third, the occupant of the pulpit, who (as Ruskin said) has 'thirty minutes to raise the dead in', and fourth, the architectural symbolism of the church as a ship and the bishop as its pilot.[21]

Union Chapel is an extraordinary building. It is a profoundly Reformed space, designed (as were the Huguenot temples) with the twin aims of hearing and seeing. The acoustics are exceptional, both for the spoken word and music. Every seat is within the preacher's sight-line, and every member of the congregation can see the preacher. The relationship between the individual and God made present in Scripture and preaching is at once direct and intensely personal, yet also collective. The rippling flow of pews through the octagonal space forces the congregation to be aware of each other as they sit under the Word and rise to sing their praises. It is Protestantly individual yet as collective as Catholicism.

The Victorian rediscovery of Gothic let image back into Reformed space, at least in stained glass windows. Union Chapel had 30 stained glass windows, the gift of a benefactor. Cubitt had little control of them, but he makes sparing use of images – angels flying in the rose windows above the arcades. His materials were fine – polished granite, Yorkshire stone, encaustic tiles, polished marble, all nicely judged to produce a harmonious effect.

The second building, erected some ten years later, is the chapel of Mansfield College, Oxford, which the German theologian Friedrich Heiler once called 'the most Catholic place in Oxford'.[22] Mansfield is a quiet triumph of non-conformist Gothic by Basil Champneys. Champneys was an Anglican, the son of a Dean of Lichfield. His legacy includes some of the best nineteenth-century university buildings – the Rylands library in Manchester, the Dutch Revival buildings at Newnham College, Cambridge, the old Cambridge Divinity School and Oxford's Indian Institute. He made Mansfield Chapel a symphony of stained glass and statues. Aniconic it is not. The chapel faces north, and the north window represents Christ in glory surrounded by St Paul, the apostles and the great figures of the Old Testament. But more interesting are the east and west windows and the statues between them. Added in 1906 after a benefaction, they are a wonderfully ecumenical collection of the saints of God – representatives of the Greek and Latin churches, the medieval church, the Puritan tradition, and the eighteenth century, all looking down on the worshipping congregation.[23]

As a building it is both a cultural and a spiritual statement. Culturally, as has often been acknowledged, it represented the 'alternative' world of English dissent reaching an intellectual and social maturity, becoming part of the

Arnoldian dream. Less fully noted is the manner in which it spoke of the quiet confidence of a Reformed tradition able now to present itself as both Reformed and Catholic, and unafraid of Catholic methodology. The saints are back, around the walls and in the windows, yet not all saints. Of the Henrician Reformation there is not a trace.[24] It is a long way from the Charenton 'temple', but there has been no diminishing of core Reformed principles. The building is designed so that the congregation are all within the preacher's eyeline, its plan longitudinal. This too is a place for a congregation to be together, a collective in praise. There seems to be one fundamental change – a pulpit placed to one side, with a central communion table. However, the reason was pragmatic and thoroughly Reformed – it was better acoustically. Nonetheless, it was serendipitous, for it anticipated the recovery of balance between Word and Sacrament which would be one of the central discoveries of the Calvinist revival of the mid twentieth century.

Social and political space

Reformed spirituality is about public space as well as liturgical space, about the 'theatre' of God's glory, the world. It is about building a city of the saints, creating an academy of vocations, and therefore it is about social concern and political life (in the sense of the life of the *polis*). If Calvin's first great achievement was his codifying of the 'true' way of understanding the world in the *Institutes*, his second was Geneva, the social and political correlative of the *Institutes*. The latter was meant to reflect the former; social life was to embody God's glory.[25] God was to be found in ordinary everyday places in ordinary everyday lives. The Anglican poet George Herbert wrote:

> Teach me my God and King
> In all things thee to see,
> And what I do in anything
> To do it as for Thee.

That spelt revolution. Calvin's Geneva generates passion and disagreement. Opinion remains divided whether the reformation of manners which he achieved in the city was a manifestation of 'the most perfect school of Christ since the apostles' (as John Knox believed) or an exercise in despotic totalitarianism. A balanced understanding has become more possible since the publication of the full records of the consistory in 1996. It was certainly a regime which scrutinised people's lives closely. Roughly one in eight of Geneva's citizens appeared before the consistory by 1560. However, it is important not to let a few melodramatic and absurd cases cast a false impression of its work. William Monter's analysis of its work between 1564 and 1569 shows that it was preponderantly concerned with social relationships – with lying and quarrels, both within the family and beyond. Such cases far outnumber 'fornication and lubricity'.[26]

The consistory emerges as a cross between a court, an educational institution and a counselling service. Robert Kingdon, the editor of the consistory records, noted:

> It really tried to assist everyone in the city-state to live the kind of life it thought God intended people to live. Nobody in Calvin's Geneva could complain of the kind of 'anomie', or complete and hopeless anonymity, that is such a curse in so many big cities in to-day's world.[27]

Calvin's ordering of social and political life was intended to bear witness to the reality of God's love, to reflect God's glory in God's proper theatre, the world. That meant nothing other than the establishment of a new way of social cohesion, and the laws of the state and the work of the consistory were ways of achieving that. The internalised Gospel was made visible in social behaviour, in care and concern, and holy awe that all life was lived under the gaze of God. This is true 'visibility', and the birth of a political aesthetic.

In the hands of Luther and then Calvin, vocation turned from being a calling out of the world into the religious life to a calling into the world. Luther's rediscovery of the doctrine

of the priesthood of all believers did not (as widely misunderstood) mean that anyone could do anything in church.
The Reformers were in fact very conservative in their
understanding of ministry. In terms of function, sacrificing
priest was replaced by preaching minister, and the role of the
laity remained roughly the same. What they did discover was
much more important: that the believers corporately were a
priestly body. Christians lifted their own space and time to
God, and let God into their own space and time. This
democratising of the priestly work was spelt out by Calvin in
his theology of vocation. God, wrote Calvin,

> has appointed duties for every man in his particular way
> of life. And that no-one may thoughtlessly transgress his
> limits, he has named these various kinds of living 'call-
> ings'. Therefore each individual has his own kind of living
> assigned to him by the Lord as a sort of sentry post so that
> he may not heedlessly wander about throughout life.[28]

Although Calvin's theological logic is compelling, this is not a
biblical concept. In vain will we look in Scripture to find God
calling anyone to be a merchant or even a healer. Rather, God
calls individuals to particular God-given tasks. The fact that
Paul was a tent-maker was incidental; his calling was to be an
apostle. Nonetheless, this new insight of the Reformers proved
itself potent, for the concept of vocation was to lie behind the
evolution of the professions, and there can be no denying the
experiential reality which compels some people towards ded-
icating their lives to medicine or teaching. Calvin's theology of
vocation sanctified work: 'who sweeps a room as for thy law/
makes that and the action fine.' It was, as Herbert noted, the
elixir, the philosopher's stone that turned ordinariness into
the material of God's kingdom. Here, for Calvin, was pastoral
assurance that the activities and work of lay people in their
space and time mattered to God, and that God could be glorified in their activities.

It is an irony that, thanks to Troeltsch and Weber, Calvinism is linked in the popular mind with the rise of

capitalism, for Calvin himself would have been horrified by the thought of acquisitive economic individualism. His commentaries abound with warnings about the corrosive power of wealth, and its attendant spiritual dangers. Any blessings we enjoy are divine gifts, intended by God to be shared with our neighbours for the common good. We are stewards of what has been given to us, so what matters is being diligent stewards.[29]

Beauty and ethics are intertwined in Calvin's thinking. God's gifts are things of beauty that are meant to be enjoyed. They are for our good:

> if we ponder to what end God created food, we shall find that he meant not only to provide for necessity but also for delight and good cheer ... Has the Lord clothed the flowers with the great beauty that greets our eyes, the sweetness of smell that is wafted upon our nostrils, and yet will it be unlawful for our eyes to be affected by that beauty, or our sense of smell by the sweetness of that odour?[30]

Of course not. The beauty of creation is to be enjoyed and delighted in. Yet sound proportion is essential. The gifts should direct our attention to the Giver, and thanksgiving to 'the Author' for 'his kindness towards us' should direct our enjoyment. That kindness is towards all, and therefore our response to it should be ethically responsible: 'Where is our gratefulness toward God for our clothing if in the sumptuousness of our apparel we both admire ourselves and despise others ...?'[31] However, Calvin suggests, earthly possessions need to be viewed through the lens of eternity. Delight in the temporal should not distract the believer from the proper work of the cultivation of the soul. More importantly, all that we have is held in trust. We are simply stewards of the earth, and one day we must give account of that stewardship. There is here the kernel of a theology of simplicity, of walking gently on the earth, and living simply that others may simply live. The moral rhetoric Calvin employs to explore this is very much of its age, contrasting frugality with ostentation, moderation with excess, yet hidden in its midst is a brilliantly creative economic insight. God 'approves no other distribution of good things than one joined with love'.[32]

The social attributes of discipleship – diligence, hard work, moderation, honesty – may well have contributed to the rise of capitalism and the growth of Western individualism, but that was not the kind of society that Calvin dreamt of. His ideal world is one in which love prevails and the good things of earth are shared open-handedly. A Reformed spirituality is therefore one which is politically and economically responsible, which seeks to see the beauty of God reflected in the ways in which societies order themselves and people treat each other.

A social spirituality: three contrasting examples

R. W. Dale was minister of Carrs Lane Congregational Church in the heart of Birmingham for over 40 years (1854–95). He was first and foremost a preacher, one of the 'pulpit princes' who dominated the landscape of Victorian evangelicalism. His recipe for successful preaching (according to his Yale lectures on the subject) was seven to eight hours reading per day, 'and a wife posted at the study door, armed with a bayonet to keep out intruders'.[33] But Dale's study was no ivory tower. He was the great exponent of the municipal or 'civic' Gospel, a man of the world. He was a member of the committee that welcomed Garibaldi to Birmingham. He led the campaign to open the governing body of King Edward's school (the city's leading school) to non-Anglicans and eventually became its bailiff (or chair). On the wider political stage, he spoke in favour of extension of the franchise, raised funds for freed slaves after the American Civil War, and built a base of considerable influence in the city. When Joseph Chamberlain was adopted as the Liberal candidate for Birmingham in 1874, one London newspaper noted that he had Dale's support, 'and the will of Mr Dale is the will of Birmingham.'[34]

In true Reformed style, Dale eschewed any division between the sacred and the secular. Life was sacred, and everything therefore fell under the purview of the preacher, for the law of Christ applied to everything. Politics itself was a sacred art, and the well-being of society was a moral responsibility for the Christian. Some of his friends found his spirituality hard to fathom. Canon O'Sullivan, the Vicar-General of the diocese, once said to Dale after a School Board meeting, 'Dale, when do you mean to quit politics and look after your soul?' Dale's son and biographer continues:

> The precise words of the reply cannot be recalled, but this was their substance: 'I have given my soul to Christ to look after ... He can do it better than *I* can; my duty is to do His will, and to leave the rest with Him.'

That was the basis of his argument that ministers should be involved in politics, and his urgent pleas that members of Carrs Lane should involve themselves in the political life of their city. Dale once helped a Quaker friend, Alderman White, win one of the roughest wards in the city:

> Ten days ago he rose in the Council. He was able to say that he had visited every street, every court in his ward. He told an appalling story of the condition of the people in that ward ... He spoke of squalid homes ... destructive to health, and rendering all high moral Christian life impossible. He submitted to the Council an elaborate scheme for sweeping away all the wretched district at a cost of four and a half millions. The Council accepted the proposal unanimously. Now I believe that my friend was trying to get the will of God done on earth as it is done in heaven just as much when he was fighting St Mary's ward, just as much when he was speaking in the Town Council, as when he was teaching his Bible Class on the Sunday morning.

This was the genesis of the 'municipal gospel':

> sweeping away streets in which it was not possible to live a healthy and decent life; ... making the town cleaner and brighter; ... providing gardens and parks and music; ... erecting baths and free libraries, an art gallery and a museum, ... good water supplied without stint at the lowest possible level.[35]

It was the rationale behind Chamberlain's programme of the 1870s, but for all its political sophistication, Calvin would have recognised that this was 'no other distribution of good things than one joined with love'.

It was an attempt to let God's beauty be reflected in social and political space. If Dale was concerned about social space, he knew that it was created by individuals, and that integrity was essential to the reality of discipleship and godly living. He expected a worldly spirituality to characterise his congregation, one lived out amongst the dangers and opportunities of a rapidly expanding commercial city. In one powerful sermon, 'The necessity of doing the will of God', Dale explores the morality of a trustee who 'borrows' trust money to cover a short-term cash-flow problem, and of a society treasurer who 'borrows' some of his society's public money for his own purposes. He then turns to clerks who 'borrow' £10 or £20 of their employer's money to pay their rent, and shopkeepers who 'borrow' from the till, and continues:

> But when we 'borrow' a little money from any man without asking him to lend, the borrowing ought to be called by a much uglier name. In all those cases the crime is committed under the resolution to replace the money. The resolution conceals the face of the criminal act, as a mask conceals the face of a burglar or highwayman; but the burglar is still a burglar and the highwayman is still a highwayman though he wears a mask; and the mask of 'good resolution' to be honest at some future time does not change the character of the criminal act committed to-day. We must *do* the will of God if we are to enter into heaven.[36]

Doing the will of God, in the sense of creating godly social space, has always exercised the Reformed, from Calvin's Geneva to the Pilgrim Fathers to the struggle against apartheid and the fight for human rights. The way the Reformed behave is governed by what they believe. The tradition's heavy stress on sin and its in-built realism about human frailty and fallenness provided potent material for one of its most significant twentieth-century thinkers. From the mid 1930s to the mid 1950s, Reinhold Niebuhr (1892-1971), the professor of social ethics at Union Theological Seminary in New York, spent his summers at the village of Heath in Northern Massachusetts. He frequently led worship at Heath Union Church, and it was for them that he wrote what has become one of the best known of modern prayers about doing the will of God: 'God, give us grace to accept with serenity the things that cannot be changed, courage to change the things that should be changed, and the wisdom to distinguish the one from the other.' It was later published in a booklet of prayers that the Federal Council of Churches published for army chaplains, and was later adopted and adapted by Alcoholics Anonymous (with Niebuhr's permission). It was a prayer born in crisis years, and it epitomises the realism of Niebuhr's social ethics.

Dale and the creators of the municipal Gospel were not unmindful of individual sin, but they had little conception of social sin, and genuinely believed that it was possible to build a better world. In the wake of the carnage of the First World War, the rise of totalitarian regimes of the left and right, and the impact of the industrial production line, such optimism was hollow. It was Reinhold's brother, Richard (1894–1962), the professor of theology at Yale, who famously characterised liberal theology as 'A God without wrath brought men without sin into a kingdom without judgement through the ministrations of a Christ without a cross.' But it was Reinhold who laid bare its ethical paucity in *Moral Man and Immoral Society* (1932) and in the two-volume *The Nature and Destiny of Man* (1941, 1943), where he used a series of dialectical paradoxes (e.g. saint and sinner, subject of history and

shaper of history) to explore what human beings are. Niebuhr's 'Christian realism' took social sin seriously. Like the
Old Testament prophets before him, especially his favourite,
Amos, he understood human nature to oscillate between self-
interest and the interest of the other, but with the former
prevailing in social groups, whether of political or economic
interests. Any system of creating social space therefore
depends on systems of checks and balances which will keep
power under control. Realism is 'the disposition to take all
factors in a social and political situation, which offer resist-
ance to established norms, into account, particularly the
factors of self interest and power'. It is Christian because it is
seen through the spectacles of the paradoxes of Christian
theology – the finite and the infinite, the kingdom of God and
the contingency of history.[37] Justice is therefore an essential
component of love:

> International peace, political and economic justice, and
> every form of social achievement represent precarious
> constructs in which the egoism of man is checked and yet
> taken for granted; and in which human sympathy and
> love must be exploited to the full and yet discounted ...
> Community must be built by men and nations sufficiently
> mature and robust to understand that political justice is
> achieved, not merely by destroying, but also by deflecting,
> beguiling and harnessing residual self-interest and by
> finding the greatest possible concurrence between self-
> interest and the general welfare.[38]

Yet, politics is penultimate for Niebuhr. Political and social life
cannot be properly appreciated without an understanding of
the grace of God, which Niebuhr sees in the providential
ordering of history, 'by which God makes the wrath of man
praise him, and transmutes good out of evil', and in the
experience of forgiveness. God has the power to 'negate and to
wipe out the corruption of egoism that all our actions betray',
and it is that resting in the goodness of God which produces
true peace, 'the religious peace of knowing that a divine mercy

accepts our loyalty to Christ despite our continued betrayal of him.'

That recognition of common sinfulness produces a deep humility, which is the foundation of a common humanity and strivings towards political peace and a just world order: 'Reconciliation with even the most evil foe requires forgiveness; and forgiveness is possible only to those who have some recognition of common guilt.' The social and political journey is towards the kingdom of God, which will always remain 'fragmentary and corrupted' in history. Yet that perspective is vital because 'It gives us a fulcrum from which we can operate in history. It gives us a faith by which we can seek to fulfil our historic tasks without illusions and without despair.' All can be servants of the kingdom:

> Martyr, prophet and statesman may each in his own way be servant of the Kingdom. Without the martyr we might live under the illusion that the kingdom of Caesar is the Kingdom of Christ in embryo and forget that there is a fundamental contradiction between the two kingdoms. Without the successful prophet, whose moral indictments effect actual changes in the world, we might forget that each moment of human history faces actual and realisable higher possibilities. Without the statesman, who uses power to correct the injustices of power, we might allow the vision of the Kingdom of Christ to become a luxury of those who can afford to acquiesce in present injustice because they do not suffer from it.[39]

Niebuhr was sometimes accused, even by his own brother, of losing touch with the transcendent aspects of his faith. His was certainly a worldly spirituality, born of his observation of the cramped and confined lives of his car-worker parishioners in Detroit. It passed by way of radical socialism and pacifism to his lonely and powerful opposition to American isolationism, and a continuing radical critique of American foreign policy up to his death. Yet, however 'worldly' it became, it always circled back to the God whose kingdom would one day come, the wisdom to distinguish those things that can be changed from those that cannot, and the courage to change those that should be changed. This was worldly spirituality at its most robust and its edgy best.

In 1969 Reinhold Niebuhr published one of his last articles, 'The King's Chapel and the King's Court', in a journal he had been instrumental in founding, *Christianity and Crisis*. It was a polemical attack on Richard Nixon's establishment of a Sunday service at the White House, and on Billy Graham who preached at the first service. Niebuhr shared Amos's abiding suspicion of religion. The God of Amos took no delight in solemn assemblies and demanded that 'justice roll down like waters and righteousness like an ever-flowing stream' (Amos 5:21, 23–4). This was a favourite text, Niebuhr noted, of Martin Luther King, who used it in his 'I have a dream' speech. It was 'unfortunate', Niebuhr continued, that he was murdered before he could be invited to the White House.

> But on second thought, the question arises: would he have been invited? Perhaps the FBI, which spied on him, had the same opinion of him as Amaziah had of Amos. Established religion, with or without legal sanction, is always chary of criticism, especially if it is relevant to public policy. Thus J. Edgar Hoover and Amaziah are seen as quaintly different versions of the same vocation – high priests in the cult of complacency and self-sufficiency. Perhaps those who accept invitations to preach at the White House should reflect on this, for they stand in danger of joining the same company.[40]

If the 'beauty' of Reformed social and political space is expressed principally in terms of justice in Niebuhr's work, it reunites with Calvinist aesthetics in John de Gruchy's reflections on the nature of beauty in the context of the South African struggle against apartheid. De Gruchy belongs to a long Reformed tradition which finds much of its spiritual dynamic in social activism. In the South African context that stretches back to John Philip, a Scottish Congregational missionary with the London Missionary Society whose Calvinist theology led to a determined stance for native rights against the interests of colonial settlers in the 1830s. Such eminent opponents of apartheid and shapers of the new South Africa as Tiya Soga, Albert Luthuli and Beyers Naude were fed by that same tradition.[41] It is all the more interesting, then, that it is from South Africa that de Gruchy pleads for the place of art in Reformed spirituality.

The beginning of his theological exploration was rooted in the politics of apartheid, and a growing awareness that it was not only unjust but ugly, and an ugliness reflected particularly in the architectural divisiveness that surrounded him. He summons D. H. Lawrence (himself the product of a Congregational childhood) in his 1929 essay 'Nottingham and the Mining Country' as a witness to the ways in which the 'moneyed classes' of Victorian England condemned their workers to 'ugliness, ugliness, ugliness: mean and formless and ugly surroundings ... The human soul needs actual beauty even more than bread'.[42]

Calvin, de Gruchy reminds us, had interesting things to say about civic architecture and town planning because he was concerned about social space. He had interesting things to say about beauty too:

> Did [God] not endow gold and silver, ivory and marble, with a loveliness that renders them more precious than other metals or stones? Did he not, in short, render many things attractive to us, apart from their necessary use?[43]

De Gruchy is both deeply committed to, and perceptively critical of, the Reformed tradition. He acknowledges that beauty and art have been at best peripheral concerns of the Reformed, with the honourable exception of two great Congregational theologians, Jonathan Edwards and P. T. Forsyth, and the abiding interest of Dutch and American neo-Calvinists. But theology is an ecumenical enterprise, so the journey inevitably passes by way of the Catholic Hans von

Balthasar. De Gruchy issues a timely challenge to the Reformed to retrieve the arts, for 'I have ... become convinced that art belongs to the soul of the church and that a church that neglects it is in danger of losing its soul.'[44]

The Reformed and art – Rembrandt and van Gogh

The Reformed have excelled at understanding the Word rationally, but the Word was incarnate, human, imaginative, creative. Jesus created word pictures with the deft economy and craft of a poet, and knew what it was to fashion wood with his hands – Joseph was, after all, a carpenter. The Word includes the imaginative and the creative, because human beings are makers and dreamers as well as doers and listeners.

It is therefore worth recalling that Calvin saw a clear function for the visual and plastic arts in the social realm. He understood artistic abilities to be the gift of the Holy Spirit.[45] All arts came from God and could bring pleasure.[46] They had a legitimate and important place in the divine economy, but that place was the public square and the home, not the sanctuary. That explains why the arts could still flourish in Reformed countries. If representations of God were forbidden by Scripture, and images were excluded from the sanctuary, portraiture and landscape remained as significant and viable subjects for the Reformed, and it is no surprise that these were the routes through which art developed in the wake of the Protestant Reformation. The portraits of Holbein and the miniatures of Hilliard, the garden designs of the Huguenots, and the establishment of the rich landscape traditions of British and Dutch art bear witness to the Calvinist reshaping of the world.

The 'worldly' spirituality of the Reformed is not so much about internalising the biblical narrative as living it in the world. As Reformed artists handled scriptural themes, they did so from a worldly perspective, encountering the texts with a realistic freedom that was free from iconographic

control. It was in the ordinary things of life, its market-
places, landscapes, casual meetings, deep encounters and
historic turnings, that they discovered true piety.

Rembrandt van Rijn (1606–69) grew up in the religious
wars of Calvinism. Rembrandt was not a card-carrying
member of the Reformed church. When his mistress, Hen-
drickje, received an official reproach from the church for
'living in sin', Rembrandt was not summonsed because he
was not a member of the church. Indeed, his earliest bio-
graphers claim that he was attracted to the radicalism of the
Mennonites. However, there is no doubting that his intellectual and social world was largely shaped by Calvinism,
and in this sense he is a truly 'Reformed' artist, and (as his
work shows) a profoundly religious one.

A recent study of *The Anatomy Lesson of Dr Nicolaes Tulp*
(1632) suggests that it might be 'read' as showing the 'worldly'
spirituality of the Reformed. The picture shows the distinguished anatomist giving a class. Colleagues and medical
students peer eagerly over the cadaver. Tulp begins his dis-
section, unusually, with the arm, his forceps indicating the
finger-flexors. Dissections normally began with the chest and
stomach. If William Shupbach's reading is correct (and it is
inevitably disputed by art historians), he begins with the arm
because in the seventeenth century the detailed ways in which
the muscles and bones interacted, and in particular the
movements of the fingers and hands, were thought to show
the mind of God behind the design of the human body. The
triangular grouping of the figures around the corpse reinforces
the message. The man at the top of the triangle points
downwards to the body, reminding the viewer of mortality,
and Tulp responds by pointing out the muscles of the arm and
holding up his own hand. Shupbach also discovered a poem by
Caspar Barlaeus (1639) about Tulp's new anatomy theatre:

> Listener, learn yourself, and while you
> Proceed through the individual
> Believe that God is hidden in even the smallest part.

It is, as Dyrness points out, as though Rembrandt has epitomised Calvin's understanding of knowledge – know yourself,
know God. God is to be found in the world, in its intricate,
providential structuring.[47] Few artists 'knew' themselves as
intimately and thoroughly as Rembrandt, as his astonishing
series of self-portraits reveals, and few have so remarkably
known God. Rembrandt turned, in true Calvinist fashion, to
Scripture for his themes. He was the most accomplished of
biblical painters. The prodigal son was a theme that fascinated
Rembrandt. In 1636 he composed an etching of it, but then, in
1669, months before he died, at the end of a life with more than
its share of grief, he returned to the subject in a painting
which now hangs in the Hermitage in St Petersburg. It is
a breathtaking picture, of infinite compassion, composed of
sharp detail and imprecise suggestion. The prodigal is kneel-
ing into his father's embrace, and the old man bends forward,
his eyes shut, gently, tenderly letting his hands rest on his
son's shoulders. The lad's tunic is dirty and torn, his feet
scarred and bruised. This has been no easy journey home. Sin,
stupidity, and failure seem to weigh on him, and in him we
recognise ourselves. But it is the old farmer's touch that is so
telling. Serenely, peacefully, his own burden of loss lifted, the
father's touch is the touch of a parent, the blessing of a priest,
and maybe (as Simon Schama suggests) 'an act of resurrection,
a transformation of death into life'.[48]

It is an astonishing, moving exploration of the Christian
Gospel, the transformation of the world's ugliness into God's
beauty, the return of prodigal humanity to its ever-loving,
ever-forgiving Creator. Some commentators would go further.
The Dutch priest Henri Nouwen who meditated long on it,
draws attention to the hands. Rembrandt isn't simply showing us the wonder of God's grace, he is offering us a profound
insight into God's being. The left hand on the son's shoulder
is large, strong and muscular. Then compare it with the soft,
refined right hand, its fingers so much closer together, elegant and gentle:

As soon as I recognized the difference between the two
hands of the father, a new world of meaning opened up for
me. The Father is not simply a great patriarch. He is
mother as well as father. He touches the son with a
masculine hand and a feminine hand. He holds, and she
caresses. He confirms and she consoles. He is, indeed,
God, in whom both manhood and womanhood, fatherhood and motherhood, are fully present. That gentle
and caressing right hand echoes for me the words of
the prophet Isaiah: 'Can a woman forget her baby at the
breast, feel no pity for the child she has borne? Even if
these were to forget, I shall not forget you. Look, I have
engraved you on the palms of my hands.'[49]

The relationship between truth, goodness and beauty is spelt
out by the work of Christ, the ugliness of the cross transforming into the beauty of resurrection, the ugliness of sin
becoming the raw material of the beauty of redemption. Van
Gogh said in one of his letters, 'This morning I visited the place
where the streetcleaners dump the rubbish. My God it was
beautiful.'[50] Van Gogh's art can be read as an essay in 'worldly'
spirituality. The son of a Reformed minister of the rather liberal Groningen school of Dutch Reformed thought, Vincent
van Gogh (1853–90) came from a long line of Reformed ministers, so it not surprising that after six years in the art trade
(the other branch of the family's interests), he found himself
exploring a vocation to ministry. In the mid 1870s he worked
as an assistant to the Revd Thomas Slade Jones, a Congregational minister who had a boarding school first in
Ramsgate, and latterly in Isleworth in west London. It was in
the small church at Turnham Green, for which Jones was also
responsible, that van Gogh began to preach, and to do pastoral
work amongst the Sunday School children and their families.[51]
Returning to the Netherlands, he was eager to be engaged in
evangelism and ministry, and perhaps impatient with preparation for university theology entrance examinations, which
he failed. Nor did he stick long on a training course for

evangelists at Laeken, near Brussels. Instead, he took an independent initiative, and ended up as an evangelist in the Belgian mining area of Borinage between 1878 and 1880. It was here, amongst the poor, that his first vocation was eclipsed by a second, and he became an artist.

The relationship between those two vocations, between the 'first' and 'second' van Goghs, has long been the subject of scholarly debate. There are continuities and discontinuities in any spiritual journey, and in van Gogh's case they are compounded by the mental suffering and illness which plagued his last years. His exploration into himself and into God took him further and further from conventional religious practice, and more and more into the world. He had always had a reverence for nature because God could be experienced through it, and indeed, it was that reverence that prevented him taking Gauguin's advice to abandon the real world as the starting point for his art.[52] It was rather in and through the real world that he found ultimate meaning. In the midst of his ill-fated love for his widowed cousin Kee in November 1881, he wrote to his brother Theo:

> You must not be astonished when, even at the risk of your taking me for a fanatic, I tell you that in order to love, I think it absolutely necessary to believe in God. To believe in God (that does not mean that you should believe all the sermons of the clergymen and the arguments and Jesuitism of the *'bégueules dévotes collet monté'* [bigoted, genteel prudes], far from it); to me, to believe in God is to feel that there is a God, not dead or stuffed but alive, urging us toward *aimer encore* with irresistible force – that is my opinion.[53]

As he developed a new visual language in the last years of his life, he travelled towards a new perception of the God whose glory, as Calvin knew, is writ large in the 'theatre' of the world. 'If I repent anything', he wrote in 1881, 'it is the time when mystical and theological notions induced me to lead too secluded a life. Gradually I have thought better of it.'[54] As he

stepped out of seclusion, and sometimes out of sanity, that
visual language became more and more elemental: cypresses,
olive trees, colour (yellow sunflowers, dazzling suns – life
itself), starry nights, light and darkness. At its best, Reformed
theology stands firm on the ground that God cannot be tamed,
that all religion is ultimately secondary, for only the revelation
of God is truth. Like Rembrandt, van Gogh was not exactly
fitted for the conventional rules of Calvinism, even in its
Groningen form. His experiences of love contrasted only too
painfully with what he considered the hypocrisy of his father
and uncle. Like Rembrandt, though, his paintings show his
extraordinary sense of God. Religion may not have been able
to cope with him, but he was still secure within the embrace
of God.

His *Starry Night* (1889) is an essay in the meaning of light.
The dark night is lit by the starry sky, which swirls and
whirls its way across the upper two thirds of the canvas,
which is divided by undulating blue hills rising from left to
right. Nestling in the right-hand corner against the hills and
under the sky is a little Provencal village. Lights shine from
the windows of the houses, and the steeple of the church
seems to cut up above the hills and touch the sky. Light
(particularly, of course, the sun) was for van Gogh a symbol
of God,[55] and it would not be far fetched to see this picture
speaking of the love of God. But the church (and as critics
have said, this is a Dutch church – French churches from this
region don't look like this) is in total darkness. It aspires to
the light, but has no light.[56]

Starry Night has been recognised as a great work of religious art ever since it was chosen as the representative piece
of nineteenth-century religious art at an exhibition in Chicago in 1954, and feted as such by Paul Tillich and others
eager to speak of 'God beyond the church'. What they may
have missed was the Reformed melody. However tortuous his
spiritual journey, however black his depression, van Gogh's
mind was steeped in Reformed culture, and Reformed spirituality is worldly – the starry night is precisely where the

Reformed would expect to encounter God. And the church lights would be on only if worship was being conducted. Calvin expected St Peter's to be locked, just in case people should seek to escape from the God who was all around them, and constrain him to a place and a ritual. In van Gogh's case, of course, that instinct has become inextricably woven into an intellectual and theological crisis which Calvin could barely have conceived. But it doesn't invalidate the instinct, and it shows, as the Reformed were slowly realising, that art has a place not only in the home or the gallery, but in the sanctuary, because art is profoundly religious, for it both creates and questions meaning.

Back in the sanctuary

The tradition which began in iconoclastic Zurich eventually reached van Gogh's Arles. It was a long journey. It changed the way in which the world was to see and hear things. The triumph of the ear in worship turned the eye outwards to the world, there to discover the God who had broken down all barriers between the sacred and the secular. It was in social and public space that the Reformed slowly discerned the link between ugliness and sin, and beauty and truth, and the ways in which Christ turned the one into the other on Jerusalem's rubbish tip. If ugliness is the raw material of redemption, if the human condition can be transformed into a thing of beauty, then art has a place in the sanctuary, for art too is redemptive.

John de Gruchy challenges Reformed churches with two examples. He takes us first to one of the 'shanty churches' in the sprawling black township of Crossroads on the edge of Cape Town. During the repression, representatives of other churches were asked to come and lead prayers for justice in one of these African Initiated Churches. He was one who did, and he tells how in a damp, makeshift sanctuary, 'a young girl dressed in white entered, carrying a lit candle entwined in barbed wire which she placed on the altar'. It spoke of light amidst darkness, hope in the midst of despair. It was not 'aesthetic' but 'it transformed the shanty into a sacred place ... it was a sanctuary of "holy beauty" for those who had entered to pray and returned home to face the bull-dozers.'

His second example is the Coptic Church of St Samaan the Shoemaker at the bottom of Mokattam Hill, overlooking Cairo, where 27,000 garbage collectors scrape a living in a filthy, stinking settlement.[57] Part of an immense grotto, it is in fact a series of seven churches carved into the rocks and caves, beautiful and lavish in true Coptic style, but serving and transforming the lives of those in the community in which it is set.

Having rediscovered the theological link between beauty and truth, de Gruchy protests that 'no congregation should have to worship in a sanctuary that is unredeemed by beauty' and calls for a reawakening of 'aesthetic sensibility' within Reformed congregations. In Western countries that sensi-bility can ride on the back of architecture, for the rediscovery of Gothic in the nineteenth century led to a rediscovery of the beauty of holiness which crossed denominational boundaries. In the wake of the Oxford Movement, flowers were to be found in the aisles of Reformed as well as Anglican churches, and the stories of Scripture (and other less wholesome stor-ies) flowed down stained glass chancels which were no respecters of theological peculiarities. Even robed choirs proved infectious.

Alongside that, in the later nineteenth century Reformed scholars in Europe and America re-evaluated their own liturgical traditions and rediscovered that to be Reformed also meant to be 'catholic'. The formation of the Church Service Society in Scotland in 1865 stimulated liturgical scholarship, and in 1867 produced a significant liturgical milestone, the *Euchologion*, a book of Common Order. It went through varying editions until 1923, and although never officially published by the Kirk, it provided the order for communion at every General Assembly from 1890 to 1923.

It was a work of delightfully catholic scope, drawing from sources as diverse as Calvin, the American German Reformed Liturgy, the Book of Common Prayer, bishop Jeremy Taylor, the Liturgy of St Basil and the Unitarian Dr James Martineau. It was catholic yet not incongruous, and it held together. Its influence within Scotland, and in the wider Reformed world, was considerable. Liturgy is one of the first manifestations of ecumenism.[58]

In America John Williamson Nevin's (1803–86) attempted restatement of Calvin's eucharistic doctrine emphasised once more the importance of Holy Communion, and his work was placed on a sounder liturgical footing by Charles Washington Baird (1828–88) whose *Eutaxia, or the Presbyterian Liturgies* (1855) promoted 'good order' in American Presbyterian worship and provided them with the Communion liturgies of Calvin and Knox in English. That was a work taken forward by Henry van Dyke (1852–1933), whose *Book of Common Worship* (1905) tried to create a prayer book from the liturgical principles of the Westminster Directory.[59]

Architecture and liturgy both played their part in helping the tradition to balance the needs of eye and ear, mind and imagination better. That is a work which has continued through the twentieth century and into the twenty-first, embracing such diverse manifestations of Reformed Christianity as the Crystal Cathedral and the Iona Community. Candles are no longer automatically anathema, and slowly but surely Reformed Christians are learning that the imagination is not to be feared but nurtured. The space of the sanctuary is where the Word is heard, summoning God's people to discover God in public space. Both are holy, bridged by the beauty of truth, and that is why the aesthetics of worship matter.

5 A LOVING GOD AND A CATHOLIC PEOPLE

Although the main theme of the Reformed symphony is Scripture, a discerning listener would note the significance of the quietly repetitive minor melody of the nature of the Church. The earliest Reformed theologians thought of themselves not as sectarian thinkers, but as Catholic theologians who were part of a 'Protest'-ant movement. So it was that Bullinger could preface his *Decades* with eleven creeds of the early Church and an affirmation of the first four ecumenical councils (only omitting the fifth and sixth because he thought them repetitious). This work was a selection of 50 sermons which were intended to provide a simple statement of the Christian faith, and he spells out clearly that he believes this to be the faith of the holy, Catholic Church, and is at pains to demonstrate that continuity. Calvin himself strove tirelessly to bring about unity until it became clear that all such efforts would be unavailing, and like Bullinger, affirmed the ecumenical councils in his writings and drew extensively on the work of the early Fathers.[1] Indeed, he is rightly regarded as one of the finest patristic scholars of his day. What mattered was continuity. From the first Reformed theology was, in that sense, Catholic theology, and the Reformed churches were the Church Catholic, properly focused, and in total apostolic continuity with the patristic Church. To be Reformed was to be Catholic.

The Reformed definition of the true Church was simple and generous. It was to be found wherever the Word was truly preached and the sacraments properly administered. Even at the height of the rhetorical war between Romans and Protestants, Calvin could say, 'when we categorically deny to the papists the title of *the* church, we do not for this reason impugn the existence of churches among them.'[2]

Such a definition makes it hard to draw boundaries. The Reformed have always been Catholic, open to the authentic Church wherever it may be found. It should be the centre that matters, the God who comes in Word and Sacraments, not the circumference. Restrictions and boundaries are not a natural part of Reformed theological culture at its best. At its worst, though – and it is a fundamental weakness – boundaries become obsessively important, and Reformed culture has a tendency to splinter like glass. The causes of division range from the weighty and majestic like the spiritual independence of the body of Christ, to the absurd like the use of musical instruments in church.

In April 1552 Calvin wrote to Archbishop Thomas Cranmer, noting that the fact that 'the churches are so divided, that human fellowship is scarcely now in any repute amongst us' was 'to be ranked amongst the chief evils of our time', and, he continued, 'So much does this concern me, that, if I could be of any service, I would not grudge to cross even ten seas, if need be, on account of it.'[3]

The generous, open understanding of the Church which was characteristic of the earliest Reformed thinkers was gradually overlaid by the vicissitudes of history and the polarisation of Catholic and Protestant Europe. Faint echoes remained, though. On the eve of the dissolution of English Protestant unity in 1660, the 'presbyterian' Richard Baxter worked selflessly and tirelessly for the unity of the Church. Offered the bishopric of Hereford, he refused, 'for it will very much disable me from an effectual promoting of the Churches Peace.'[4] His work was in vain, but his witness to the true nature of Reformed ecclesiology remained. Responding to an anonymous author who complained that he did not know which party Baxter belonged to, he described himself as 'a

CHRISTIAN, a MEER CHRISTIAN, of no other Religion; and the Church that I am of is the Christian Church, and hath been visible where ever the Christian Religion and Church hath been visible'.[5]

That was the authentic Reformed voice, but it was not to be heard again until the early nineteenth century, when Calvin began to be read with new eyes.

John Williamson Nevin and the nature of Reformed piety

John Williamson Nevin (1803–66) was born in Franklin County, Pennsylvania, of Scots–Irish descent, educated at Union College and Princeton, and spent his career teaching in theological seminaries. His spiritual history is interesting. He grew up within the fellowship of the Church, and believed, in a classical Calvinist sense, that the visible Church was the medium of salvation for the baptised. 'There is no entrance into life', wrote Calvin of the Church, 'save as she may conceive us in her womb, give us birth, nourish us from her breasts, and embrace us in her loving care to the end.'[6] Cumberland Valley Presbyterianism was something of a backwater. America had moved on. Revivalism, which has its roots in New England Puritanism, was all-pervasive. As a 17-year-old college student, Nevin fell under its spell and was converted, and brought into the Church – 'as if', he later wrote, 'I had been altogether out of it before'.

Most students would have accepted that as the reality of their spiritual journey. Not so Nevin. It troubled him that the piety of his boyhood should be so cavalierly dismissed, and as a theologian he returned again and again to the subject of the Church, contrasting the 'true' Reformed experience of his childhood with the 'Puritanism' of the revival. 'Puritanising' religion, he suggests, was forever studying the soul's temperature charts, charting almost manic-depressive highs and lows. It was the kind of spirituality which Richard Baxter called 'heart accounts'. Nevin did not care for it. He

wrote of a fellow Princetonian who was blessed with visions
and voices, yet returned home a wreck, left the faith,
became a novelist, then a lawyer, before turning again to
ministry and ending up a suicide.

The other form of piety was objective, concentrating on
the action of God, finding its sustenance in the Creed and the
Westminster Shorter Catechism. It sought assurance in the
external, and was wary of gauging the health of the soul by
the chart of the emotions. They, after all, were part of the
package of fallenness, and not to be trusted.

It was clear where his preference lay, and he set out to
discover why. For revivalism, the suspect upstart on the
Reformed scene in Nevin's eyes, 'Conversion is everything,
sanctification nothing. Religion is not regarded as the life of
God in the soul, that must be cultivated in order that it may
grow, but rather as a transient excitement to be renewed.'
The older system was rather a new life, grounded in Christ,
the 'organic root' of the Church. Here was a Reformed theologian reforming, moving behind assumption, journeying *ad
fontes*. Nevin was a church historian, and within his discipline, the source he was most concerned about was not
Scripture but Calvin. His achievement was to confront
the Calvinists with Calvin. His chosen battlefields – the
nature of the Church and the Eucharist – went to the heart
of the tradition. Rome, said tradition, was anti-Christ. Not
so, said Nevin – the spirit of sectarianism is. The Eucharist
is but a memorial meal, said tradition. Not so, said
Nevin. When we gather at the table, we are united to Christ
through the power of the Spirit and feed on the very body
and blood of the Lord. And he provided a copious apparatus
of footnotes to show precisely what Calvin had said. Anything
between the cross and 1517 is wrong, tradition implied.
Nonsense, said Nevin – the Church Catholic is one organism
in Christ.

Reformed orthodoxy in America, dominated by the might
and wealth and intellectual power of Princeton Seminary,
was scandalised. It took the great Charles Hodge (1797–1878)

two years to review *The Mystical Body*, so upset was he by his pupil's departure from Princetonian orthodoxy.

When Nevin wrote, he was on the staff of the little German Reformed seminary at Mercersberg. His colleague there was Phillip Schaff, the indomitably energetic church historian and biblical scholar. Schaff and Nevin were both widely read in German theology and history, Catholic as well as Protestant. Their theology – Mercersberg theology, as it become known – was part of the sudden resurgence of high church ideas in the 1830s and 1840s which manifested itself in Britain in the Oxford Movement and the Scottish Disruption and in the renewal of Lutheranism in Germany.

Although Nevin's influence was minimal, his sensitive spiritual antennae registered the first stirrings of questions about the nature of catholicity, and therefore Christian unity, and the shape of Christian community which were to be of central importance during the twentieth century.[7]

The Reformed understanding of Christian community

The Reformed, along with all Protestants, had reacted decisively against monasticism in the sixteenth century. Some reasons were laudable, others spurious. The very concept of a religious order seemed in contradiction to justification by faith. The idea of religious discipline was thought to undermine the liberty of the Gospel, which was for every believer, but above all for the Reformed, the whole Christian community was expected to live a godly life. Calvin rejected the monastic ideal in order that the world might be the arena for disciplined, godly living.

The spread of Reformed Christianity in the sixteenth century was accompanied by a longing for the reformation of manners. Comparative studies of Scottish, French, Dutch and Swiss disciplinary bodies reveal interesting contextual divergences. Whereas Scottish kirk sessions seemed preoccupied with sexual misconduct, French consistories were more concerned with handling conflicts between neighbours, doctrinal matters and having recourse to magic and 'popish practices', whereas the metropolitan Amsterdam Kerkeraad (although much exercised by adultery and sexual sins) found itself giving sustained attention to the problem of bankruptcy throughout the seventeenth century. For all the variety, though, two overriding concerns can be discerned: that people fulfilled their duties to God, and to their neighbours – in other words, both tables of the ten commandments.[8] Their concern with the first table was initially about establishing the new Reformed system, teaching people the Lord's Prayer and the Apostle's Creed, letting the new pattern of liturgy and churchgoing take root, and dealing with the vestiges of Catholic devotion. Churchgoing was enforced because it was central to the creation of a new spirituality.

The second table was social, political and economic territory which the Church shared in varying proportions with the State. After a careful survey of the scholarly evidence, Philip Benedict concludes that during the seventeenth century Reformed discipline in some measure helped reduce feuding, interpersonal violence and sexual misconduct, whilst at the same time strengthening marriage and the nuclear family. Some social historians understand this as an exercise in social control. In part it was, but it was much more than that. To those who were members of these churches, it was evidence that they belonged to one another in Christ, and within that community, bore responsibility for each other. The monastery had, in effect, become the whole Church. There were genuine similarities between the Reformed tradition and monasticism. Both strove for simplicity, sincerity and pure behaviour. Where the Reformed tradition expressed itself in a Congregational polity, the parallels were all the more compelling. Congregational churches were self-governing; so were Cistercian abbeys, and the Premonstratensians were described by one of their historians as 'independent congregations'.[9] Whatever the similarities, however, it is clear that most of the Reformed, indeed most Protestants, completely repudiated monasticism.

Writing about the same time that Nevin was discovering Calvin's catholicity anew, the Danish Lutheran Soren Kierkegaard noted in his *Journal*:

> There is no doubt that the present time, and Protestantism always, needs the monastery again; there is no doubt that it should exist. The 'monastery' is an essential dialectical fact in Christianity and we need to have it there like a lighthouse, in order to gauge where we are ... If there is to be true Christianity, in every generation, there must be individuals to meet that need.[10]

It was surely no coincidence that two of the most significant experiments in Christian community of the twentieth century were the creations of two very different Reformed ministers – George MacLeod and Roger Schutz.

George Macleod and the Iona Community

George MacLeod was probably the most significant Scottish church leader of the twentieth century. He was the son of Sir John Mackintosh MacLeod, MP for Glasgow Central (1915–18) and Kelvingrove (1918–22) and his wife Edith, the daughter of a wealthy Unitarian mill-owner. His lineage was peppered with distinguished Highland ministers, a significant number of whom had served as Moderators of the General Assembly.

Educated at Winchester and Oriel College, Oxford, like all good Scottish aristocrats in Edwardian England, George MacLeod absorbed elitism without question. He read law at Oxford, but his career was interrupted in 1914, and he returned to Scotland to enlist as an officer in the Argyll and Sutherland Highlanders. He had a good war. He survived, which was blessing enough in itself, but many of his school friends did not. He was awarded the Military Cross for conspicuous bravery at Ypres in an encounter that saw 15 out of 20 fellow officers and 330 out of 400 men in his battalion slaughtered. The French added the Croix de Guerre Avec Palmes for a later battle. The realities of killing dawned on

him. They did not make him a pacifist – that was to come
later – but touching the deepest realities of living turned
him from law to theology and the ministry of the Church of
Scotland. New College Edinburgh was followed by Union
Seminary in New York. After America came an assistantship
at St Giles Cathedral Edinburgh. Privilege seemed to be
working its inevitable magic. MacLeod seemed set to rise
with effortless ease. Eloquence and glamour marked his every
step, as he moved from St Giles for four years as assistant
at St Cuthberts in Edinburgh's fashionable West End. The
church was crammed full. Fashionable young women crowded
the pews, and George became known as the 'Rudolf Valentino
of the pulpit'. In 1930 he accepted a call to Govan, on the
south bank of the Clyde, to shipyards hit by recession and
poverty, with an unemployment rate of just over 60 per cent.

Those surprised by the move had read but the surface.
They had missed the George Macleod who was captivated by
notions of community learnt from Tubby Clayton and TocH,
who had found his real ministry amongst the street kids of
Edinburgh, and discovered for himself the sinfulness of the
two nations of rich and poor. Under the privileged skin of the
aristocrat was the anger of one who was to learn acutely and
well what it meant to be a troubler of Israel. Govan was to be
the laboratory in which he was to discover whether the
Gospel could touch urban, industrial Scotland. It was the
poverty and inequality which hurt:

> Once I entered a house where a woman was suffering
> from puerperal fever and the family were sitting around
> silent and dismayed. 'Get hot water bottles,' I cried, 'six of
> them' – and nobody moved. You see they hadn't the money
> for one, let alone six hot water bottles. There was no
> health insurance. Only one doctor could be relied on for
> midnight calls among ten thousand people, and he, the
> saint, was a coloured man. I saw a lad of ten crying with
> the toothache. 'Oh yes', said the mother, 'he can get it
> pulled. But not till Friday when the dole's paid out.'[11]

He gave of himself without question, and of his own fortune without qualm, setting up accounts at the local pharmacists for those who did not have the money to pay for their own medicines. Energy, creativity and passion flowed. The number of worshippers rose steadily, but it was all too much and energy gave way to depression and breakdown. It was, suggests his biographer, a delayed reaction to the war and its aftermath. His way of coping with the horror of war was to view it as a national purgation, the chance to do a new thing, to build a new tomorrow, a land indeed fit for heroes. The reality was Govan with three million unemployed, the dole cut and means-testing introduced. Even he, with all his gifts, background and style, could not build the kingdom single-handed. So it was that at Easter in 1933 he found himself in Jerusalem, convalescing on a trip to the Holy Land. The turning point was the early morning Easter service of the Russian Orthodox Church. The strangeness, pageantry and holy seriousness of it gripped him. He wrote in his journal:

> When the Patriarch was heard arriving, the gates of the sanctuary were flung open – two young priests, with flowing hair and beards, rushed out to meet him – the choir sang the Responses – Actions – they all entered the sanctuary – they all rushed out – *Christ is risen* – Candles! Quick procession – every movement was sprightly. Out of the church we all ran behind them – lighted candles in our hands – round the church three times singing, in the crisp star-laden night. Here was the answer to Modern Criticism! *Of course, Christ had risen!*[12]

Easter had found him. He had been given a new way of seeing, a way which held in tension the political, the theological and the personal. Through Orthodox worship he had found what it truly meant to be Reformed. Just like Barth wrestling with Romans in the manse at Safenwil, MacLeod was confronted with the reality of the risen Christ. This was not a fact to be fitted into an edifice of facts gleaned from other places and other disciplines. This was *the* fact which relativised all other

facts. This was the starting point for living. MacLeod returned
to Govan determined to make a new beginning, to create a new
community of faith, the first step on a path to the 'godly
commonwealth':

> People are beginning to see that a new social order must
> be born if the majority of men are to share and enjoy the
> wealth and plenty that even now science has put within
> their grasp. The problem of the coming days is going to be
> how best to arrive at that Christian Commonwealth which
> alone can satisfy our legitimate aspirations ... Before we
> can deal with the details of 'how to share' (Politics) we feel
> we must capture the 'will to share' (Religion). If that be so,
> has not the Church of Christ a mighty challenge before it,
> if its eyes be open in days like these?[13]

Time and again in Reformed history, from Calvin's Geneva in
the 1540s to New England a century later and Thomas Chalmers's Glasgow in the 1810s, this word had been heard – a
word of action, reformation, political transformation for the
sake of the Gospel. MacLeod began by launching a mission of
friendship in the parish, run with military precision, each
home visited twice, supported by a chain of prayer, combined
with community action as unemployed craftsmen were drafted
in to create a community garden around the war memorial
next to the church. It was remarkably successful. The parish
system, he concluded, could work, if only the Church of Scotland were to adopt the correct methods to make it work.
Throughout the turbulent thirties, MacLeod continued with
imaginative ministry at Govan Old Parish. One precursor of
the future was the rebuilding of Fingalton Mill, three miles
above Barrhead on the edges of Fenwick Moor, by the unemployed, to act as a holiday centre for Govan's poor. It was in the
increasing polarisation of politics, caught between Moseley
and Marx, that MacLeod began to grope his way towards a
new theory of pacifism and peacemaking. That was balanced
by a redefining of the Scottish Reformed tradition in the light
of what he considered to be Scotland's Celtic heritage. He was

a great spinner of myths, a hypnotic caster of spells, and none too careful an historian. What he argued for – frequent communion, liturgy, daily worship, congregational re-sponses – was neither Celtic, nor Roman, but an integral part of a Reformed tradition which had been overly biased by Puritanism. In 1937 Glasgow University honoured his contribution to the religious life of the city by awarding him a DD. The following March Hitler invaded Austria, and in the April, George MacLeod resigned from Govan.

MacLeod was later to say that the Iona Community began when he was street preaching in Govan and a down-at-heel little man asked him, 'Do you think all this religious stuff can save?' Then a few weeks later he received a request to visit a man called Archie Gray in hospital. He did so and found the man who had asked him that question, dying of starvation. Out of 21 shillings a week he was sending seven shillings and sixpence to a ne'er-do-well brother in Australia, and he'd left a household full of the unemployed because he felt he'd been eating too much of the rations. He was bitter about the Church not because it was lying, but because it was speaking the truth and did not mean what it said.[14] The Iona Com-munity was MacLeod's attempt to get the Church to put its money where its mouth was. What attracted him now were experiments in Christian community – the Moravian Bru-derhof in the Cotswolds, Bonhoeffer's experiments in theo-logical education in Germany, and of course, TocH. His eye lit upon Iona.

Iona was and is a remarkable place. MacLeod famously called it a 'thin' place, a place where the division between heaven and earth was tissue-thin. In the sixth century it was the home of Columba and his community, and the saint's burial place. Scottish and Norwegian kings found their final resting place there, including (said the myths) MacBeth and Duncan. Benedictine monks founded an abbey there in the twelfth century, making it again a centre of learning and prayer. In the eighteenth and nineteenth centuries it became the focus of Romantic pilgrims as they journeyed through the

Highlands, and there was (so legend had it) a prophecy by the dying Columba:

> Iona of my heart, Iona of my love,
> Instead of monks' voices there shall be lowing of cattle:
> But ere the world comes to an end
> Iona shall be as it was.[15]

In 1899 the Duke of Argyll had handed the ruins of the cathedral to a public trust. The trust deed records the ecumenical generosity of the Duke who wished all churches to be able to worship there. In a neat manoeuvre he outflanked the local minister and kirk session, for the trust deed also forbade them to have any part in the management of worship in the cathedral, except for their own services. The trustees were the great and the good of the Kirk and the universities.

By 1910 the Abbey was beautifully restored. What confronted George MacLeod in the 1930s was an exquisite church set in the midst of ruins. It seemed a parable of the Church's position in society – a fine sanctuary in the midst of a dysfunctional community. He believed that the days of one-person ministry were numbered. Only teams could handle the complexities of society. Iona could become the base for a community within the Church of Scotland which could become a spearhead for the Church's work in urban ministry. Given what he considered to be the collapse of the Puritan paradigm in the Church of Scotland, he was eager to consider Celtic and Catholic models of monastic community as alternatives. It was audacious and brave – a high-risk strategy – and at the age of 42 he staked everything on it.

Ordinands, ministers and craftsmen formed an extraordinary community, living a disciplined life, setting about the rebuilding with the divines acting as the labourers. It was a crucible which formed true community and true worship. Then war intervened and the focus shifted, for many of the incipient community went off to fight, or act as chaplains, or join reserved occupations. MacLeod's pacifism created controversy – he was banned for two years from broadcasting

on the BBC, for example – yet the shift of emphasis made
Iona an international symbol. Visitors from far and wide
came to Iona to take part in short educational courses which
reflected the concerns of the Community. That was the birth
of Iona, the great pilgrim centre. The focus of the Community's work shifted to the mainland, to Edinburgh. As the war
intensified, MacLeod found himself more and more margin-
alised and misunderstood – accusations of communism,
catholicism and pacifism rained on him.

One day, sitting on a hill on Iona, he was greeted by a
complete stranger who asked him if he was successful yet. 'It
depends what you mean,' said MacLeod. 'Don't you know
what success is?' asked the stranger. 'Success is hearing the
voice of God no louder than thunder in distant hills on a
summer day.' And he went on walking.

In September 1940 a Swedish ship had to jettison its cargo
of wood, and it floated all the way to Mull, directly opposite
Iona – all the right length for George's building plans.
'Whenever I pray', he said, 'I find that the coincidences
multiply.'[16]

George MacLeod was never an easy man – prophets aren't
smooth. In the immediate post-war period the Community's
relationship with the Kirk was turbulent. It took 13 years to
work out a constitutional arrangement that brought it within
the discipline of the Church. In the midst of it he caused a
storm by accepting a call back to Govan Old Parish whilst
remaining Leader of the Iona Community. Glasgow Presbytery refused to concur, and after two years of acrimonious
debate on the floor of Assembly, Assembly decided in favour
of the Presbytery. Yet behind all of that, there was huge
respect for MacLeod's integrity, for his passion for people,
and his unstinting giving of himself to support the poor and
cast aside. He even flew back from a lecturing tour in
America to appear in court on behalf of a disturbed young
man whom he had taken under his wings in his Govan days.
The cost was considerable, for the young man was accused of
murdering a former Youth Secretary of the Iona Community,

and as part of his evidence MacLeod had to admit that he had known that the murdered man had homosexual tendencies. That outraged 1950s Scotland, and more obloquy descended on the Community.

However, two years later the Kirk's ambivalent attitude to its most turbulent priest was writ large when he was elected Moderator of the General Assembly for 1957. George and the Community remained on the radical edge, but from then on there was no doubting that their work was recognised and embraced by the wider Church.

George MacLeod was an intuitive rather than a professional theologian. He told a famous story about the boy who threw a stone through a stained glass window which knocked out the letter 'e' in 'Highest', so that the text then read: 'Glory to God in the High St.' He went on:

> Holiness, salvation, glory are all come down to earth in Jesus Christ our Lord. Truth is to be found in the constant interaction of the claim that the apex of the Divine Majesty is declared in Christ's humanity. The Word of God cannot be dissociated from the Action of God. As the blood courses through the body, so the spiritual is alone kept healthy in its interaction in the High St.[17]

MacLeod's God was active, involved, getting his hands dirty, part of the rough and tumble of the contingent. MacLeod expected to discover God in the city streets because God had walked Jerusalem's streets in Jesus the Christ. His theology began with God's encounter with the world in Jesus Christ. In one of the loveliest of his Iona prayers, entitled 'Man is Made to Rise', he wrote of Christ:

> You are released, resplendent, in the loving mother,
> the dutiful daughter, the passionate bride
> and in every sacrificial soul.
> Inapprehensible we know You, Christ beside us.
> Intangible, we touch You, Christ within us.
> With earthly eyes we see ourselves, dust of dust, earth of

the earth; fit subject at last for the analyst's table. But
with the eye of faith, we know ourselves all girt about of
eternal stuff,
>   our minds capable of Divinity
>   our bodies groaning, waiting for the revealing,
>   our souls redeemed, renewed.
Intangible we touch You, Christ within us.[18]

Reformed spirituality and thought about God since the
Enlightenment falls into two patterns: the Barthian, which
begins with God's revelation; and the Schleiermacherian,
which looks inward to discover within ourselves a God-
consciousness. George MacLeod, natural mystic that he was,
found himself in the latter company. Barth, he once muttered,
was easier to pronounce than apply. Indeed, he found himself
more attracted to Rudolf Steiner than Barth, which worried
his critics. What he lacked in systematic consistency, he made
up for in mystic insight and prophetic understanding. God's
immanence was more apparent to him than God's transcendence. His Christ was to be found in the depths of every soul,
the very stuff of divinity in each person. His Christ was also
cosmic, the centre of everything that was created:

>   In You all things consist and hang together:
>   The very atom is light energy,
>   The grass is vibrant
>   The rocks pulsate.[19]

His definition of Christian orthodoxy was 'a belief in a Person
who always has many things to tell us but we cannot hear
them now. He has given us the Spirit of Truth that shall guide
us into all the truth: a sentence that implies that we must keep
moving.'[20]

Passionately convinced of the centrality of Jesus Christ, he
was wary of any system, especially those Reformed ones
which seemed to him to have strangled the soul out of
Scottish Christianity. Yet for all that, he knew that he had
been formed by it, its 'virus' lurking still in 'the marrow of

our psyche'.[21] Part of that was the unhelpful heritage of the image of the heavy-handed disciplinarian God, but part was blessing too, for when

> I can accept ... that no man has seen God at any time, and that Christ has declared him as SPIRIT – God is a Spirit and they that pray to Him must pray to Him in Spirit and in Truth – then I am delivered by the sheer reality of the situation. Christ above, beside, within, beneath me, creates a sort of atomic field of relationship.[22]

He was not worried about the loose threads and contradictions in his thought. The Reformed tradition provided the granite beneath his feet, but it made a pilgrim path, not a prison. The 'atomic field of relationship' spoke of his understanding of integration and integrity – of worship with politics, prayer with action, devotion with lifestyle. The material and spiritual were inseparable. Life was a whole. 'The true mark of Christian spirituality,' wrote MacLeod, 'is getting one's teeth into things. Painstaking service to mankind's most material needs is the essence of spirituality.'[23] Such activism is profoundly Reformed. The Calvinist virus was more tenacious than MacLeod realised. This is the spirituality of vocation – the master mason and the carpenter rebuilding the abbey refectory, the trades unionist struggling for justice, the politician fighting for multiculturalism, the doctor bringing health, the financier creating employment. It is engaged and worldly. It does not recognise a division between the sacred and the secular because one of its principal tenets is that all ground is holy ground, for (as MacLeod memorably put it), 'Christ was not crucified on a cathedral altar between two candlesticks, but on a city rubbish dump between two thieves.'

MacLeod understood perfectly the theological dynamics of vocation. His was a 'worldly spirituality'. Every time could be alight with the glory of God. All creation can be offered up to God by God's priestly people. That is what the spirituality of vocation is about. George MacLeod knew that, and he prayed:

Almighty God who hast called all believers to a full vocation, so that Thy priesthood is in every home and place of
work, we lift to Thee Thy ministers at factory bench, at
desk, in kitchen and wherever a witness can be made.

Visit them in their times of prayer, that all who work
beside them may take note that they have been with
Jesus, and by the standard that they see in them may be
rebuked or comforted till they seek of us and of them our
secret as it is in Thee.[24]

The Iona Community, which has about 250 members, 1500
Associate Members and 1400 Friends worldwide, still seeks
to live out that spirituality of vocation.[25] It is an eclectic community – ecumenical, lay and ordained, men and women, by no
means all from Scotland. The 'glue' which binds it together is its
Rule, offering guidance for living a spiritually integrated life. It
has been more or less in its present form for the past 30 years. It
has five components. First, and most important, is the daily
devotional discipline of prayer and Bible reading, and the community produces its own prayer lectionary and 'directory', the
Miles Christi, so that the same prayers are said in the Abbey
itself and across the Community. That grounding in God's story
then flows out into the other four disciplines – sharing and
accountability for the use of money, time-planning, the pursuit
of peace and justice, and meeting together to be mutually
accountable.

It is a call to responsible and balanced living. Members are
expected to tithe their personal disposable income after their
basic needs and any exceptional circumstances have been
taken into account, and the tithe is then divided between the
work of the Community, local congregations, organisations
that work for peace and justice, and particular causes re-
commended by members.

The rule about time is said to have its origins in the early
days of the Community when the craftsmen doubted the
ministers' ability to do an eight-hour shift. Now, *Miles
Christi* notes:

we are all asked to plan our time in such a way that equal 'weighting' is given, not simply to work, but equally to leisure, to time for family, to developing skills or acquiring new ones, to worship and devotion, to voluntary work – and to sleep!

Spiritual integrity requires balance, as Benedict realised when he organised the monastic day between devotion, study and work. It is attention to this balance of life that creates the space for the essentially political task of the fourth discipline, seeking peace and justice. The life of the Community is built up by the fifth discipline, a commitment to meet together, both on Iona and in more local Family Groups.[26]

If the Rule draws from both monastic and Reformed spiritual traditions, the worship of the Community has developed the synthesis of Celtic and Reformed understandings which was so characteristic of MacLeod himself, and that in turn has influenced the ways in which the Church of Scotland and other Reformed churches have developed their liturgical lives. Communities like Iona and Taizé have profound reach, and are helping to form the tradition they grew from.

Brother Roger, Taizé and Grandchamp

The Iona Community was launched in 1938. The First World Conference of Christian Youth met in Amsterdam from 24 July to 2 August the following year. Standing under a banner proclaiming the theme of the conference – *Christus Victor* – MacLeod gave the main address, 'Can Men Be Brothers?' He inserted into it a description of the launching of the Iona Community. Sitting in his audience were Roger Schutz and Ray Davey, founders respectively of Taizé and Corrymeela.[27]

Roger Schutz (1915–2005) later recalled how impressed he had been by MacLeod's address, and how it had inspired him in his work with refugee children in Vichy France and the journey towards Taizé.[28] Like MacLeod, he was a child of the manse, one of a long line of pastors. He was born in

Provence, near Neuchâtel, in 1915 where his father Charles was ministering. Like MacLeod, he saw the significance of Christian community, but whereas Macleod saw it as a way of bringing Church and world together, he saw it as a way of bringing divided Christians together.

From childhood Schutz had been painfully aware of the divisions between the Catholic and Protestant communities. His own family was unusual. His maternal grandmother was so saddened by the sight of Christian killing Christian in the Great War, that she decided she should seek reconciliation within herself, so despite coming from a long line of Protestants, she started worshipping in a Catholic church. Similarly, Schutz remembered his father going into a Catholic church to pray silently. It was therefore not surprising that when he had to go away to secondary school, his parents opted for him to lodge with a poor Catholic widow, Madame Bioley, whom they judged needed the income. Roger was later to say it was his experience of his two 'families', the one Protestant, the other Catholic, which shaped his ecumenical vision. Catholics, he knew, were good people, and Christian division was a scandal. The Schutzes were also deeply attracted to Mother Marie Angelique Arnaud's (1591–1661) reform of the Cistercian community at Port-Royal, which so influenced Pascal and the development of Jansenism. Roger seems to have been more attracted by the intensity and influence of the life of that small community than by its theology.

After surviving TB in his late adolescence, he read theology at Lausanne and Strasbourg, experimenting with forms of community life whilst still a student. He had two principles in mind – that religious orders at their best have always been open to the world, and that monasticism is the heart of the Church. He was later to explain to Olive Wyon:

> I was convinced that the *strength* of monasticism was fundamental; that it was a great force, and that the Church could do great things with bodies of men, united by vows, to a lifelong fidelity ... I was convinced of this. So

> I felt that I must restore to the Church the element which had been rejected.[29]

That was a remarkable decision, for there had not been such a community within Protestantism for 400 years. He chose to begin his experiment in a house in Taizé in 1940, a few miles south of the Vichy demarcation line. This was dangerous territory, criss-crossed by refugees, and Roger's vocation included radical hospitality. All were welcome. Jews and Christians, French, Swiss and Germans were equally welcome. He was denounced to the Gestapo in November 1942, but mercifully was not in the house himself. No one knows what became of the refugees who were. He was unable to return until 1944. In the meantime he completed his studies with a thesis on Benedictine monasticism, and began living the common life in a flat near Geneva Cathedral with some enthusiastic friends – Max Thurian, Pierre Souverain and Daniel de Montmollin.

After the liberation of France in 1944, Roger and his friends returned to Taizé. At first it was a hard, difficult ministry. Poverty was rife. The local population didn't understand what they were trying to do, and the welcome they gave to German prisoners was resented. They took in orphan boys, and Geneviève Schutz (Roger's sister) joined them to care for them properly, eventually becoming 'Maman' to 20 of them. It was a symbol both of Roger's long-term commitment to the area, and the community's determination to serve the poor.

The community grew very slowly. In 1948 they sought permission from the local bishop for a *simultaneum* for the scarcely used village church, a method of allowing a Catholic church to be used for non-Catholic worship. The bishop passed the request to the papal nuncio, Angelo Giuseppe Roncalli, later Pope John XXIII. He responded with alacrity, and the brothers held their first service there in Pentecost 1948. The following Easter seven brothers took their vows in that little church.

Roger's thinking about monasticism was to develop from an 18-page pamphlet that he wrote in 1941, through the *Introduction to Community Life* (1944) to *The Rule of Taizé* (1952/3). He said, 'I began with the three words that encapsulated the spirit of the beatitudes: joy, simplicity and mercy. In them was the essence of the gospel.'[30] From that grew a life grounded in the Reformed discipline of letting Scripture soak into the soul, and a prayerful openness to Christ. The *Introduction* states, 'Through your day let work and rest be quickened by the Word of God. Keep inner silence in all things and you will dwell in Christ. Be filled with the spirit of the beatitudes, joy, simplicity and praise.'

Taizé was not a 'normal' religious community. It was made up, initially, of Protestants, but Protestants who felt it was their calling to be what Roger termed 'a parable of reconciliation'. They were neither a traditional monastic order, nor a church, but something unique, a living parable. 'Christ', Roger said, 'has in a sense called us to recapture the image of a reconciled church ... a small reflection of what that communion is for everyone, a small reflection of the church, that is constantly reconciling itself.'[31] A very Reformed understanding of the provisionality of the Church can be detected behind this vocation. The brothers therefore resisted the attempts of the French Reformed to turn them into a church, and made strenuous efforts to stop Pius XII using Papal Infallibility to promulgate the doctrine of the Assumption in 1950. They remained in a lonely ecumenical wilderness in the 1950s until Roncalli was elected as Pope John XXIII in 1958 and Vatican II ushered in undreamt-of possibilities. 'Taizé', said the new Pope when he met Roger, 'that little springtime.' And so they remain, an image of what they pray will one day be. As Roger put it on a visit to Rome in 1980: 'without being a symbol of repudiation for anyone, I have found my own identity as a Christian by reconciling in myself the current of faith of my Protestant origins with the faith of the Catholic church.'[32] Under his leadership Taizé's ecumenical influence has been far reaching. He forged notable

friendships with such varied church leaders as John XXIII,
Paul VI, Patriarch Athenagoras of Constantinople and Eugene Carson Blake of the World Council of Churches. The
first Catholic brothers were professed in 1969, after Cardinal
Marty authorised Catholics to join the Community. There are
now over 100 brothers, from Catholic and various Protestant
backgrounds from more than 25 nations. Brother Roger was
tragically murdered in the Church of the Reconciliation at
Taizé in August 2005. The Community continues under the
guidance of his designated successor, Brother Aloïs.

Ecumenism is not primarily about the unity of the Church,
but of the whole of God's precious *oikoumene*, of which
humanity has stewardship. Taizé's spiritual witness is
therefore expressed not simply in worship, but in social and
political solidarity. Since 1951 the Community has had 'fra-
ternities' scattered across the world, where two or three
brothers live in community, bearing witness to Christ's presence and joy in places of poverty and tension.

An unexpected and unplanned ecumenical 'gift' was the
development of Taizé as a place of pilgrimage for young
people, attracted perhaps by the worship, perhaps by the
simplicity of the place, yet finding it a place of meeting, with
each other and with God. The brothers developed a ministry
of listening to their young guests, and in 1974 Roger built a
'Council of Youth' on those foundations, in which he explored
with 40,000 young people from across the world and across
the churches the relationships between contemplation,
prayer, social commitment and politics. That in turn led to
the 'Pilgrimage of Trust on the Earth', a multi-level
exploration of what it might mean to spread Christ's peace
and reconciliation across the world.

The still point of this spiritual dynamo is worship. 'Taizé
appeals to the ear', wrote one scholarly visitor, and there is a
sense in which its repetitive, gentle chanting, often of scriptural texts, pays tribute to Calvin's insistence that the people
should sing the Psalms.[33] This music, and the thoroughly
biblical structure and form of the liturgy (which owes much

to Max Thurian), have helped spread Taizé's influence world-
wide. As they have done so, they have shown how the
Reformed understanding of the Word can be held within a
cradle of deep, prayerful silence.

The women's community at Grandchamp near Neuchâtel,
which is now closely related to the Taizé community, and
shares its liturgy, has its origins in a three-day retreat for
women from the Swiss Reformed Church in 1931 – the first
ever held in that church.[34] Five years later one of those
women opened a house of prayer in Grandchamp. The community grew slowly, and its ministry of prayer and retreat
gained recognition within the life of the Reformed Church. By
1944 they recognised that something new and exciting was
taking place through their work, and they invited one of the
original retreatants, Geneviève Micheli, to give them some
leadership. She did, and was installed as Mother Superior in
1952. The following year they adopted the Taizé Rule, and
vowed to show 'their common unity in thought, prayer and
action' with their fraternal community. There are now about
60 sisters world-wide, drawn not only from Switzerland, but
elsewhere in Europe, Africa and Asia. Although their prime
ministry is the round of prayer, devotion and retreat at
Grandchamp and the Sonnenhof at Gerterkinden in the
German-speaking canton of Bâsle, they too (like the Taizé
brothers) live in small groups in Israel, Algiers and the
Netherlands, seeking to be a presence of friendship and
prayer.[35]

The Church, for the Reformed, is defined not in terms of
doctrine or structure, but of the activity of God in Word and
sacraments. That has enabled the Reformed to recognise the
ministries, sacraments, and memberships of other churches,
and it is little surprise, therefore, that the Reformed have
found themselves partners in many church unions, from the
United Church of Canada in 1925, to the Church of South in
India in 1947, to the Protestant Church in the Netherlands in
2004. As significant, if not more, has been the Reformed
rediscovery of community in the differing forms of Taizé,

Grandchamp and Iona. Unity is not just about structures, but relationships, between God, God's people, their neighbours, and creation.

Unity, for the Reformed, is to be found in creation's relationship to the Creator, and it is therefore not an end in itself but an integral part of God's mission of reconciling the world to himself in Christ. As the Dutch Reformed missiologist David Bosch noted, the quest for Christian unity 'is part of the new search for wholeness and unity and for overcoming dualism and dividedness. It is not the result of lazy tolerance, indifference and relativism but of a new grasp of what being Christians in the world is all about.'[36]

God's love knows no bounds. There is mission, and there is Church, because God loves people.[37] Near the end of John Updike's novel *The Centaur*, the main character, George Caldwell, a high-school teacher, remembers walking with his minister father down a dangerous street on a Saturday night errand. The parish is a run-down industrial town dominated by a sulphur works and the men are getting drunk in the bars:

> From within the double doors of a saloon there welled a poisonous laughter that seemed to distill all the cruelty and blasphemy in the world, and he wondered how such a noise could have a place under the sky of his father's God ...

And then he recalls

> his father turning and listening in his backwards collar to the laughter from the saloon and then smiling down to his son, 'All joy belongs to the Lord.'
>
> It was half a joke but the boy took it to heart. *All joy belongs to the Lord.* Wherever in the faith and confusion and misery, a soul felt joy, there the Lord came and claimed it as his own; into bar rooms and brothels and classrooms and alleys slippery with spittle, no matter how dark and scabbed and remote, in China or Africa or Brazil,

wherever a moment of joy was felt, there the Lord stole and added to His enduring domain ...[38]

God is there before us, a generous giver of lavish grace. The unity of the Church lies in that grace, which is why the Reformed seek to be a catholic people.

NOTES

Introduction

1. John Leith, *An Introduction to the Reformed Tradition* (Atlanta, John Knox Press, 1977), p. 34.
2. Philip Sheldrake, *Spirituality and History* (London, SPCK, 1991), p. 36. These paragraphs are heavily dependent on Sheldrake.
3. Sandra Schneiders, 'Christian Spirituality: Definition, Methods and Types' in Philip Sheldrake (ed.), *The New SCM Dictionary of Christian Spirituality* (London, SCM Press, 2005), pp. 1–6; David Cornick, 'Post-Enlightenment Pastoral Care: Into the Twentieth Century' in G. R. Evans (ed.), *A History of Pastoral Care* (London, Cassell, 2000), pp. 362–79.
4. Gordon Wakefield, 'Spirituality' in Gordon Wakefield (ed.), *A Dictionary of Christian Spirituality* (London, SCM Press, 1993), p. 362.
5. A glance at the history of the hymnbook during the twentieth century amply confirms this perception.
6. Sheldrake, *Spirituality and History*, op. cit., pp. 50–52.
7. Rowan Williams, *The Wound of Knowledge: Christian Spirituality from the New Testament to St John of the Cross* (London, Darton, Longman and Todd, 1979), p. 2.
8. Howard Rice, *Reformed Spirituality – An Introduction for Believers* (Atlanta, Westminster John Knox Press, 1991).
9. John Oman, *Grace and Personality* (Cambridge, Cambridge University Press, 1925), pp. 14–15.
10. Rowan Williams, *Why Study the Past? The Quest for the Historical Church* (London, Darton, Longman and Todd, 2005).
11. Ibid., pp. 32–9, 49, 65–71.
12. Ronald Fergusson, *George Macleod, Founder of the Iona Community* (Collins, London, 1990), p. 103.

Chapter 1: Who Are the Reformed?

1. David Cornick, 'The Reformation Crisis in Pastoral Care' in G. R. Evans (ed.), *A History of Pastoral Care* (London, Cassell, 2000), pp. 223–52, at p. 228, following P. N. Brooks, 'Martin Luther and the

Pastoral Dilemma' in P. N. Brooks (ed.), *Christian Spirituality: Essays in Honour of Gordon Rupp* (London, 1975), pp. 95–119.

2. Gordon Rupp, *Patterns of Reformation* (London, Epworth Press, 1969), p. 88.

3. For Karlstadt, see Rupp, op. cit., pp. 49–149.

4. Carlos Eire, *War Against the Idols* (Cambridge, Cambridge University Press, 1986), p. 58.

5. Ibid., p. 59.

6. Ulrich G. Gabler, *Huldrych Zwingli: His Life and Work* (ET: Ruth Gritsch, Edinburgh, T. & T. Clark, 1987), pp. 38–40.

7. Eire, op. cit., p. 76.

8. Ibid., p. 76.

9. Ibid., p. 85.

10. Ibid., p. 83.

11. Gabler, op. cit., pp. 39–40; Alexander Ganoczy, *The Young Calvin* (ET: David Foxgrover and Wade Provo, Edinburgh, T. & T. Clark, 1988), pp. 180–81.

12. J. Wayne Baker, *Heinrich Bullinger and the Covenant: The Other Reformed Tradition* (Athens, Ohio, Ohio University Press, 1980), p. 11.

13. Ganoczy, op. cit., p. 108.

14. William J. Bouwsma, *John Calvin, a Sixteenth Century Portrait* (Oxford, Oxford University Press, 1988), p. 24.

15. Howard Hageman, 'Reformed Spirituality' in Frank Senn, *Protestant Spiritual Traditions* (Mahwah, New Jersey, Paulist Press, 1986), pp. 55–80, see esp. pp. 71–2; Elsie Anne McKie, 'General Introduction' in *John Calvin: Writings on Pastoral Piety* (Mahwah, New Jersey, Paulist Press, 2001), p. 5.

16. Calvin, sermon 50 on Job, cited in Bouswsma, op. cit., p. 161.

17. Calvin, sermon 181 on Deuteronomy (OC28 col. 697), as cited in Bernard Cottret, *Calvin, a Biography* (ET: M. Wallace MacDonald, Edinburgh, T. & T. Clark, 2000), p. 345.

18. William Bouwsma, 'The Spirituality of John Calvin' in Jill Raitt, Bernard McGinn and John Meyendorff (eds.), *Christian Spirituality: High Middle Ages and Reformation* (London, SCM Press 1989), pp. 318–34, at p. 324.

19. These paragraphs rely on Lukas Vischer, 'The Reformed Tradition and its Multiple Facets' in Jean-Jacques Bauswein and Lukas Vischer (eds.), *The Reformed Family World-wide – a Survey* (Grand Rapids, Eerdmans, 1999), pp. 1–35.

20. David Weir, *The Origins of Federal Theology in Sixteenth Century Reformation Thought* (Oxford, Oxford University Press, 1990), p. 52.

21. Ibid., p. 5.

22. David Cornick, 'The Reformed Elder', *Expository Times*, vol. 98 (1986/7), pp. 235–40.

23. Dairmaid MacCulloch, *Reformation: Europe's House Divided 1490–1700* (London, Penguin, 2003), p. 310; Euan Cameron, *The European*

Reformation (Oxford, Oxford University Press, 1991), pp. 376–81; Carl Bangs, *Arminius: A Study in the Dutch Reformation* (Nashville, Abington Press, 1971), p. 94.

24. Bangs, op. cit., pp. 129–30.
25. J. L. Price, *The Dutch Republic in the Seventeenth Century* (Basingstoke, MacMillan, 1998), pp. 100–104.
26. Bangs, op. cit., pp. 176–85.
27. The Accra confession (2004), 'Covenanting for Justice in the Economy and the Earth'.
28. Brian Gerrish, 'J. W. Nevin on the Church and the Eucharist' in *Tradition and the Modern World: Reformed Theology in the Nineteenth Century* (Chicago, University of Chicago Press, 1978), p. 50.
29. *Joint Declaration on the Doctrine of Justification*, Preamble, para. 5, www.vatican.va/roman.curia/pontifical_council/chrstuni/documents/rc_pc_chrstunit_doc_3110199_cath-luth-joint-declarataion_en_html; accessed 20.07.07.

Chapter 2: A Speaking God and a Listening People

1. Karl Barth, *Prayer*, 50th anniversary edn, ed. Don E. Saliers (Louisville, Westminster John Knox, 2002), p. 14.
2. Ibid., p. ix.
3. Elsie McKie (ed.), *John Calvin: Writings on Pastoral Piety* (Mahwah, New Jersey, Paulist Press, 2001), pp. 135–77.
4. Mark Noll, *America's God: From Jonathan Edwards to Abraham Lincoln* (Oxford, Oxford University Press, 2002), p. 378.
5. R. S. Wallace, *Calvin's Doctrine of the Word and Sacraments* (Edinburgh, 1953; this edn Scottish Academic Press, 1993), p. 113, quoting Calvin's commentary on John 3:2: '*crasse et plebeio stylo*'.
6. P. T. Forsyth, *Positive Preaching and the Modern Mind* (London, Independent Press, 1907), pp. 4, 53–4; David Peel, *Reforming Theology* (London, United Reformed Church, 2002), p. 209.
7. H. H. Farmer, *The Servant of the Word* (London, Nisbet & Co., 1941), p. 29.
8. Quoted in G. H. Barbour, *The Life of Alexander Whyte D.D.* (London, Hodder and Stoughton, 1923), p. 290.
9. Walter Brueggemann, 'Preaching as Re-imagination', *Theology Today*, vol. 52, no. 3 (Oct. 1990), pp. 313–30.
10. Walter Brueggemann, *Finally Comes the Poet: Daring Speech for Proclamation* (Minneapolis, Fortress Press, c. 1989), pp. 15ff.
11. Brueggemann, 'Preaching as Re-imagination', op. cit.
12. Brueggemann, *Finally Comes the Poet*, op. cit., p. 85.
13. That point is well made by Beverley Zink-Sawyer, 'The Word Purely Preached and Heard: The Listeners and the Hermeneutical Endeavour', *Interpretation*, vol. 51, no. 4 (Oct. 1997), pp. 342–58, on whom this paragraph relies. Unfortunately we know far more about what

preachers thought listeners ought to hear than what listeners actually heard.

14. Harry Stout, *The New England Soul: Preaching and Religious Culture in Colonial New England* (Oxford, Oxford University Press, 1986), pp. 3–10.

15. B. L. Manning, 'Effectual Preaching: The Reflexion of One Hearer' in *A Layman in the Ministry* (London, Independent Press, 1942), pp. 135–51.

16. G. H. Barbour, *The Life of Alexander Whyte D.D.*, op. cit., p. 317.

17. Hughes Oliphant Old, *Worship Reformed According to Scripture* (Louisville, Westminster John Knox Press, 2002), p. 100.

18. McKie, op. cit., p. 6.

19. Horton Davies, *Worship and Theology in England: From Andrewes to Baxter and Foxe, 1603–1690* (Princeton, Princeton University Press, 1975), pp. 408–12.

20. Isaac Watts, *A Guide to Prayer* (abridged and edited by Harry Escott: London, Epworth Press, 1948), pp. 38–9.

21. Murdo Ewan Mcdonald, 'D. M. Baillie – As a Student Saw Him' in David Fergusson (ed.), *Christ, Church and Society: Essays on John Baillie and Donald Baillie* (Edinburgh, T. & T. Clark, 1993), pp. 281–7, at p. 285.

22. Ronald Fergusson, 'Introduction' in George MacLeod, *The Whole Earth Shall Cry Glory* (Iona, Wild Goose Publications, 1985).

23. MacLeod, *The Whole Earth Shall Cry Glory*, op. cit., p. 8.

24. Alec Cheyne, 'The Baillie Brothers: A Biographical Introduction' in David Fergusson (ed.), *Christ, Church and Society: Essays on John Baillie and Donald Baillie* (Edinburgh, T. & T. Clark, 1993), pp. 3–37, at p. 8.

25. John Baillie, *Christian Devotion: Addresses by John Baillie* (Oxford, Oxford University Press, 1962), p. 23.

26. John Baillie, *A Diary of Private Prayer* (Oxford, Oxford University Press, 1936).

27. Watts, op. cit., p. 78.

28. www.wts.edu/resources/heidelberg.html – accessed 19.05.05.

29. John Calvin, *Institutes of the Christian Religion*, ed. J. T. McNeil (ET: F. L. Battles, Philadelphia, Westminster Press, 1960), III.xx.1.

30. Ibid., III.xx.2.

31. Ibid., III.xx.4.

32. Ibid., III.xx.6.

33. Ibid., III.xx.17–20.

34. Ibid., III.xx.28.

35. Ibid., III.xx.29.

36. Ibid., III.xx.34.

37. Ibid., III.xx.40.

38. Ibid., III.xx.36.

39. Ibid., III.xx.37.

40. Ibid., III.xx.38.
41. Ibid., III.xx.41.
42. Barth, op. cit., pp. 32–4.
43. Olive Wyon, *The School of Prayer* (London, SCM Press, 1943), p. 21.
44. Calvin, op. cit., III.xx.42.
45. Barth, op. cit., pp. 34–41.
46. Wyon, op. cit., p. 22.
47. Calvin, op. cit., III.xx.43.
48. Barth, op. cit., pp. 41–2.
49. Wyon, op. cit., p. 24.
50. Barth, op. cit., pp. 28–9.
51. Wyon, op. cit., p. 58.
52. Barth, op. cit., pp. 44–5.
53. Wyon, op. cit., p. 58.
54. Calvin, op. cit., III.xx.44.
55. Barth, op. cit., pp. 49–51.
56. Calvin, op. cit., III.xx.45.
57. Barth, op. cit., p. 55.
58. Ibid., p. 58.
59. Wyon, op. cit., p. 60.
60. Ibid.
61. Calvin, op. cit., III.xx.46.
62. Barth, op. cit., pp. 59–64.

Chapter 3: A Choosing God and a Chosen People

1. D. MacMillan, *The Life of George Matheson DD LLD FRSE* (London, Hodder and Stoughton, 1908), pp. 128, 179.
2. 'Preface to the Complete Edition of Luther's Latin Works' (1545) (trans. Bro. Andrew Thornton OSB) from WA, vd. 4, ed. Otto Clemen, 6th edn. (Berlin, de Gruyter, 1967), pp. 421–8, www.iclnet.org/pub/resources/text/wittenberg/luther/preflat-eng.txt, accessed 19.11.07.
3. Karl Barth, *Church Dogmatics*, II/2 (ET: Edinburgh, T. & T. Clark, 1957), p. 13; David Peel, *Reforming Theology: Explorations in the Theological Traditions of the United Reformed Church* (London, United Reformed Church, 2002), p. 159.
4. William Bouwsma, *John Calvin: A Sixteenth Century Portrait* (Oxford, Oxford University Press, 1988), p. 172.
5. John Calvin, *Institutes of the Christian Religion*, ed. J. T. McNeil (ET: F. L. Battles, Philadelphia, Westminster Press, 1960), III.xxiv.12.
6. Alan P. F. Sell, *The Great Debate: Calvinism, Arminianism and Salvation* (Worthing, H. E. Walter, 1983), p. 3.
7. Paul Jewett, *Election and Predestination* (Grand Rapids, Eerdmans, 1985), p. 86.
8. The reference is to D. J. Enright's savagely ironic lines in his 1946

poem 'Apocalypse': 'It soothes the savage doubts./ One Bach out-weighs ten Belsens.'

9. For the text see William S. Johnson and John H. Leith, *A Reformed Reader: A Sourcebook in Christian Theology*, vol. 1, *Classical Beginnings 1519–1799* (Louisville, Kentucky, Westminster John Knox Press, 1993), p. 98.

10. Ch. 3, para. 3 of the Confession. For the text see David M. Thompson, *Stating the Gospel: Formulations and Declarations of Faith from the Heritage of the United Reformed Church* (Edinburgh, T. & T. Clark, 1990).

11. George Stroup, *A Reformed Reader: A Sourcebook in Christian Theology*, vol. 2, *Contemporary Trajectories 1799–present* (Louisville, Kentucky, Westminster John Knox Press, 1993) p. 85, commenting on Karl Barth, *Church Dogmatics*, II/2, pp. 94–5, 417–19.

12. John H. Leith, *An Introduction to the Reformed Tradition* (Atlanta, John Knox Press, 1977), p. 68.

13. John L. Bell, *One is the Body: Songs of Unity and Diversity* (Glasgow, Wild Goose Publications, 2000).

14. Colin Gunton, *The Christian Faith: An Introduction to Christian Doctrine* (Oxford, Blackwells, 2002), p. 30.

15. John de Gruchy, *Liberating Reformed Theology: A South African Contribution to an Ecumenical Debate* (Grand Rapids, Eerdmans, 1991), pp. 128–9.

16. Ziauddin Sardar and Merryl Wyn Davies, *Why Do People Hate America?* (Duxford, Icon Books, 2002), p. 156.

17. De Gruchy, op. cit., p. 126.

18. Geoffrey F. Nuttall, *The Holy Spirit in Puritan Faith and Experience* (Oxford, Blackwells, 1947), p. 23.

19. As cited in Gordon Mursell, *English Spirituality: From Earliest Times to 1700* (London, SPCK, 2001), p. 360.

20. N. H. Keeble, *Richard Baxter: Puritan Man of Letters* (Oxford, Oxford University Press, 1982), pp. 132–43.

21. Donald Davie, *A Gathered Church: The Literature of the English Dissenting Interest 1700–1930* (London, Routledge and Kegan Paul, 1978), pp. 28–32.

22. This reading is inspired by, and heavily indebted to, J. R. Watson's beautifully perceptive analysis of the poem in J. R. Watson, *The English Hymn* (Oxford, Oxford University Press, 1997), pp. 160–70.

Chapter 4: A Holy God and a Worldly People

1. Dairmaid MacCulloch, *Reformation: Europe's House Divided 1490–1700* (London, Allen Lane, 2003), p. 710.

2. John Calvin, *Institutes of the Christian Religion*, ed. J. T. McNeil (ET: F. L. Battles, Philadelphia, Westminster Press, 1960), I.xi.13.

3. Ibid., I.i.2, note 5.

4. Ibid., I.iv.1.
5. Ibid., I.xi.8.
6. Ibid., I.v.1.
7. Ibid., I.v.2.
8. Ibid., I.xi.12.
9. Eamon Duffy, *Marking the Hours: English People and Their Prayers 1240–1570* (London, Yale University Press, 2006), p. 172.
10. William Dyrness, *Reformed Theology and Visual Culture: The Protestant Imagination from Calvin to Edwards* (Cambridge, Cambridge University Press, 2004), p. 59, citing the work of Lee Palmer Wandel.
11. This is a recurrent image in Calvin – *Institutes*, op. cit., I.vi.1, p. 70; for other occurrences and secondary literature, see McNeil's editorial note, p. 70, f.1.
12. Dyrness, op. cit., p. 68.
13. The following argument is heavily dependent on Dyrness's groundbreaking study (op. cit.) which has redefined our understanding of the development of the Reformed tradition.
14. Dyrness, op. cit., p. 135.
15. Ibid., p. 137.
16. http://www.studylight.org/com/mhc-com/view.cgi?book=lu&chapter=015 – accessed 26.01.07.
17. Dyrness, op. cit., pp. 76, 141.
18. Robert L. Mentzer, 'The Reformed Churches of France and the Visual Arts' in Paul C. Finney (ed.), *Seeing Beyond the Word: Visual Arts and the Calvinist Tradition* (Grand Rapids, Eerdmans, 1999), pp. 199–230, at p. 205, citing Martin Bucer.
19. Clyde Binfield, *The Contexting of a Chapel Architect: James Cubitt 1836–1912* (London, The Chapels Society, 2001), p. vii.
20. George Starr, 'Art and Architecture in the Hungarian Reformed Church' in Finney (ed.), op. cit., pp. 301–40, at pp. 309–11.
21. Binfield, op. cit., p. 55.
22. Horton Davies, *Worship and Theology in England: From Newman to Martineau 1850–1900* (Oxford, Oxford University Press, 1962), p. 56.
23. Elaine Kaye, *Mansfield College, Oxford: Its Origin, History and Significance* (Oxford, Oxford University Press, 1999), p. 80.
24. Clyde Binfield, *So Down to Prayers: Studies in English Nonconformity 1780–1920* (London, J. M. Dent and Co., 1977), p. 166.
25. Dyrness, op. cit., p. 82.
26. Philip Benedict, *Christ's Churches Purely Reformed: A Social History of Calvinism* (London, Yale University Press, 2002), p. 104.
27. Robert M. Kingdon, 'The Geneva Consistory in the Time of Calvin' in Andrew Pettegree, Alistair Duke and Gillian Lewis (eds.), *Calvinism in Europe 1540–1620* (Cambridge, Cambridge University Press, 1994), pp. 21–34, at p. 34.
28. Calvin, op. cit., III.x.6.

29. J. T. McNeil, *The History and Character of Calvinism* (Oxford, Oxford University Press, 1954), pp. 221–2.
30. Calvin, op. cit., III.x.2.
31. Ibid.
32. Ibid., III.x.5.
33. Hugh MacLeod, 'The Power of the Pulpit' in Clyde Binfield (ed.), *The Cross and the City: Essays in Commemoration of Robert William Dale 1829–1895* (London, Supplement to the *Journal of the United Reformed Church History Society*, vol. 6, Supplement no. 2, Spring 1999), p. 45.
34. A. W. W. Dale, *The Life of R. W. Dale of Birmingham* (London, Hodder and Stoughton, 1902), p. 421.
35. Ibid., pp. 399–402 (for all three quotations).
36. R. W. Dale, *The Evangelical Revival and Other Sermons* (London, Hodder and Stoughton, 1880), p. 115.
37. Larry Rasmussen (ed.), *Reinhold Niebuhr: Theologian of Public Life* (London, Collins, 1988), pp. 20–21.
38. Ibid., p. 131.
39. Ibid., pp. 133–5.
40. Ibid., pp. 272–3.
41. Graham Duncan, 'Presbyterian Spirituality in Southern Africa', *Scottish Journal of Theology*, 56 (4), 2003, pp. 387–403, at p. 400.
42. John de Gruchy, *Christianity, Art and Transformation: Theological Aesthetics in the Struggle for Justice* (Cambridge, Cambridge University Press, 2001), pp. 87–8.
43. Calvin, op. cit., III.x.2.
44. De Gruchy, op. cit., p. 254.
45. Calvin, op. cit., II.ii.15–16.
46. Ibid., I.xi.12; II.ii.16.
47. Dyrness, op. cit., pp. 211–12.
48. Simon Schama, *Rembrandt's Eyes* (London, Allen Lane, The Penguin Press, 1999).
49. Henri Nouwen, *The Return of the Prodigal Son: A Story of Homecoming* (London, Darton, Longman and Todd, 1994), p. 99.
50. Quoted in de Gruchy, op. cit., p. 78.
51. Some commentators have accepted J. van Gogh-Bonger's description of Jones as a Methodist (*The Complete Letters of Vincent van Gogh*, J. Constable, 1958–60). He wasn't, and it makes far more sense for van Gogh to have found contacts within the Reformed family. – John H. Taylor, 'Thomas Slade Jones and Vincent van Gogh: a Note', *Journal of the United Reformed Church History Society*, vol. 6 (2002), no. 10, p. 758.
52. Ann Murray, 'The Religious Background of Vincent van Gogh and its Relation to His Views on Nature and Art', *Journal of the American Academy of Religion*, vol. 66 (1978) (1), p. 66.
53. www.vggallery.com/letters/main/htm, accessed 05.05.07.

54. Quoted in Anton Wessels, *'A Kind of Bible': Vincent van Gogh as Evangelist* (London, SCM Press, 2000), p. 109.
55. Ibid., p. 130.
56. Richard Kidd and Graham Sparkes, *God and the Art of Seeing: Visual Resources for a Journey of Faith* (Oxford, Regent's Park College, 2003), pp. 196–9.
57. De Gruchy, op. cit., p. 214.
58. Davies, op. cit., pp. 92–100.
59. Hughes Oliphant Old, *Worship: Reformed According to Scripture* (Louisville, Westminster John Knox Press, 2002), pp. 142–3.

Chapter 5: A Loving God and a Catholic People

1. William Stacey Johnson and John Leith, *A Reformed Reader*, vol. 1 (Louisville, Westminster John Knox, 1993), p. xxi.
2. John Calvin, *Institutes of the Christian Religion*, ed. J. T. McNeil (ET: F. L. Battles, Philadelphia, Westminster Press, 1960), IV.iii.12.
3. As quoted in Lukas Vischer, *Pia Conspiratio: Calvin on the Unity of the Church* (Geneva, John Knox International Reformed Centre, 2000), pp. 29–30. This useful compendium brings together a wide range of Calvin's writings on unity.
4. G. F. Nuttall, 'The First Nonconformists' in G. F. Nuttall and Owen Chadwick (eds.), *From Uniformity to Union 1662–1962* (London, SPCK, 1962), pp. 151–87, at p. 182.
5. N. H. Keeble, *Richard Baxter, Puritan Man of Letters* (Oxford, Oxford University Press, 1992), pp. 23–4.
6. Brian Gerrish, 'J. W. Nevin on the Church and the Eucharist' in *Tradition and the Modern World: Reformed Theology in the Nineteenth Century* (Chicago, University of Chicago Press, 1978), p. 53.
7. For the Reformed contribution to ecumenism, see Chapter 1 above, pp. 51–2.
8. Philip Benedict, *Christ's Churches Purely Reformed: A Social History of Calvinism* (New Haven, Yale University Press, 2002), p. 474. His survey of scholarship about the exercise of discipline, pp. 460–89, is admirable.
9. G. F. Nuttall, *Visible Saints: The Congregational Way 1640–1660* (Oxford, Basil Blackwell, 1957), pp. 3–4.
10. Journal for 1847 and 1848, nos. 1123 and 711, as cited in Olive Wyon, *Living Streams* (London, SCM, 1963), p. 63.
11. Ronald Fergusson, *George MacLeod, Founder of the Iona Community* (London, Collins, 1990), p. 103.
12. Ibid., p. 109.
13. Ibid., pp. 114–15.
14. Ibid., p. 138.
15. Ibid., p. 142.
16. Ibid., pp. 182–3.

17. Ibid., p. 238.
18. George MacLeod, *The Whole Earth Shall Cry Glory* (Glasgow, Wild Goose Publications, 1985), p. 16.
19. Ibid.
20. Fergusson, op. cit., p. 192.
21. Ibid., p. 193, in a letter to Duncan Finalyson.
22. Ibid., p. 194.
23. Norman Shanks, *Iona, God's Energy: The Spirituality and Vision of the Iona Community* (London, Hodder and Stoughton, 1999), pp. 9–10. No source given.
24. MacLeod, op. cit., p. 54.
25. www.iona.org.uk – accessed 05.07.07.
26. Shanks, op. cit., pp. 56–76.
27. The Correymeela Community was founded by an Irish Presbyterian minister, Ray Davey, much later in 1964. Inspired by Iona, Taizé and the work of the Waldensian pastor Tullio Vinay's Youth Village of Agape, it predated the Troubles in Northern Ireland, but played a remarkable role in the reconciliation and healing of divided communities during the Troubles. See Ray Davey, *A Channel of Peace: The Story of the Corrymeela Community* (London, Marshall Pickering, 1993); Alf McCreary, *Correymeela: Hill of Harmony in Northern Ireland* (New York, Hawthorn Press, 1976). Its ministry continues.
28. I owe this information to the Revd Geoffrey Beck, then Warden of the Chapel of Unity at Coventry Cathedral, recalling a conversation with Prior Roger on 9 February 1967. He was also present at the Amsterdam Conference, and notes that because MacLeod's account of the founding of the Community was not in his official text, it is not recorded in the official record of the proceedings (private correspondence).
29. J. L. Gonzales Balado, *The Story of Taizé* (London, Mowbray, 1980), pp. 14–15; Kathryn Spink, *A Universal Heart: The Life and Vision of Brother Roger of Taizé* (London, SPCK, 1986), p. 15; Wyon, op. cit., p. 64.
30. Spink, op. cit., pp. 45–6.
31. Ibid., p. 69.
32. Balado, op. cit., p. 31.
33. Beldon Lane, 'The Whole World Singing: A Journey to Iona and Taizé', *Christian Century* (22 March 2000).
34. Wyon, op. cit., pp. 68–9.
35. Wyon, op. cit., pp. 68–73; www.grandchamp.org – accessed 14.07.07.
36. David Bosch, *Transforming Mission: Paradigm Shifts in the Theology of Mission* (Maryknoll, Orbis, 2001), p. 464.
37. Ibid., p. 392.
38. John Updike, *The Centaur* (New York, Knopf, 1963), p. 168, cited by John McTavish, 'John Updike and the Funny Theologian', *Theology Today*, vol. 48, no. 4, Jan. 1992, pp. 413–25.

BIBLIOGRAPHY

John Baillie, *A Diary of Private Prayer* (Oxford, Oxford University Press, 1936)

John Baillie, *Christian Devotion: Addresses by John Baillie* (Oxford, Oxford University Press, 1962)

J. Wayne Baker, *Heinrich Bullinger and the Covenant: The Other Reformed Tradition* (Athens, Ohio, Ohio University Press, 1980)

J. L. Gonzales Balado, *The Story of Taizé* (London, Mowbray, 1980)

Carl Bangs, *Arminius: A Study in the Dutch Reformation* (Nashville, Abington Press, 1971)

G. H. Barbour, *The Life of Alexander Whyte D.D.* (London, Hodder and Stoughton, 1923)

Karl Barth, *Church Dogmatics* II/2 (ET: Edinburgh, T. & T. Clark, 1957)

Karl Barth, *Prayer*, 50th anniversary edition, ed. Don E. Saliers (Louisville, Westminster John Knox, 2002)

John L. Bell, *One Is the Body: Songs of Unity and Diversity* (Glasgow, Wild Goose Publications, 2000)

Philip Benedict, *Christ's Churches Purely Reformed: A Social History of Calvinism* (London, Yale University Press, 2002)

Clyde Binfield, *So Down to Prayers: Studies in English Nonconformity 1780–1920* (London, J. M. Dent & Co., 1977)

Clyde Binfield, *The Contexting of a Chapel Architect: James Cubitt 1836–1912* (London, The Chapels Society, 2001)

David Bosch, *Transforming Mission: Paradigm Shifts in the Theology of Mission* (Orbis, Maryknoll, 2001)

William J. Bouwsma, *John Calvin: A Sixteenth Century Portrait* (Oxford, Oxford University Press, 1988)

William J. Bouwsma, 'The Spirituality of John Calvin' in Jill Raitt, Bernard McGinn and John Meyendorff (eds.), *Christian Spirituality: High Middle Ages and Reformation* (London, SCM Press, 1989), pp. 318–34

P. N. Brooks (ed.), *Christian Spirituality: Essays in Honour of Gordon Rupp* (London, 1975)

Walter Brueggemann, 'Preaching as Re-imagination', *Theology Today*, vol. 52, no. 3 (Oct. 1990), pp. 313–30

Walter Brueggemann, *Finally Comes the Poet: Daring Speech for Proclamation* (Minneapolis, Fortress Press, c. 1989)

John Calvin, *Institutes of the Christian Religion*, ed. J. T. McNeil, tr. F. L. Battles (Philadelphia, Westminster Press, 1960)

Euan Cameron, *The European Reformation* (Oxford, Oxford University Press, 1991)

Alec Cheyne, 'The Baillie Brothers: A Biographical Introduction' in David Fergusson (ed.), *Christ, Church and Society: Essays on John Baillie and Donald Baillie* (Edinburgh, T. & T. Clark, 1993), pp. 3–37

David Cornick, 'The Reformed Elder', *Expository Times*, vol. 98 (1986/7), pp. 235–40

David Cornick, 'Post-Enlightenment Pastoral Care: Into the Twentieth Century' in G. R. Evans (ed.), *A History of Pastoral Care* (London, Cassell, 2000), pp. 362–79.

Bernard Cottret, *Calvin: A Biography* (ET: M. Wallace MacDonald, Edinburgh, T. & T. Clark, 2000)

A. W. W. Dale, *The Life of R. W. Dale of Birmingham* (London, Hodder and Stoughton, 1902)

R. W. Dale, *The Evangelical Revival and Other Sermons* (London, Hodder and Stoughton, 1880)

Donald Davie, *A Gathered Church: The Literature of the English Dissenting Interest 1700–1930* (London, Routledge and Kegan Paul, 1978)

Horton Davies, *Worship and Theology in England: From Andrewes to Baxter and Foxe, 1603–1690* (Princeton, Princeton University Press, 1975)

Horton Davies, *Worship and Theology in England: From Newman to Martineau 1850–1900* (Oxford, Oxford University Press, 1962)

John de Gruchy, *Liberating Reformed Theology: A South African Contribution to an Ecumenical Debate* (Grand Rapids, Eerdmans, 1991)

John de Gruchy, *Christianity, Art and Transformation: Theological Aesthetics in the Struggle for Justice* (Cambridge, Cambridge University Press, 2001)

Eamon Duffy, *Marking the Hours: English People and Their Prayers 1240–1570* (London, Yale University Press, 2006)

Graham Duncan, 'Presbyterian Spirituality in Southern Africa', *Scottish Journal of Theology*, 56 (2003) (4), pp. 387–403

William Dyrness, *Reformed Theology and Visual Culture: The Protestant Imagination from Calvin to Edwards* (Cambridge, Cambridge University Press, 2004)

Carlos Eire, *War Against the Idols* (Cambridge, Cambridge University Press, 1986)

H. H. Farmer, *The Servant of the Word* (London, Nisbet & Co., 1941)

Ronald Fergusson, 'Introduction' in George MacLeod, *The Whole Earth Shall Cry Glory* (Iona, Wild Goose Publications, 1985)

Ronald Fergusson, *George MacLeod, Founder of the Iona Community* (London, Collins, 1990)

Paul C. Finney (ed.), *Seeing Beyond the Word: Visual Arts and the Calvinist Tradition* (Grand Rapids, Eerdmans, 1999)

P. T. Forsyth, *Positive Preaching and the Modern Mind* (London, Independent Press, 1907)

Ulrich G. Gabler, *Huldrych Zwingli: His Life and Work* (ET: Ruth Gritsch, Edinburgh, T. & T. Clark, 1987)

Alexander Ganoczy, *The Young Calvin* (ET: David Foxgrover and Wade Provo, Edinburgh, T. & T. Clark, 1988)

Brian Gerrish, 'J. W. Nevin on the Church and the Eucharist' in *Tradition and the Modern World: Reformed Theology in the Nineteenth Century* (Chicago, University of Chicago Press, 1978), pp. 49–70

Colin Gunton, *The Christian Faith: An Introduction to Christian Doctrine* (Oxford, Blackwells, 2002)

Howard Hageman, 'Reformed Spirituality' in Frank Senn, *Protestant Spiritual Traditions* (Mahwah, New Jersey, Paulist Press, c. 1986), pp. 55–80

Paul Jewett, *Election and Predestination* (Grand Rapids, Eerdmans, 1985)

William S. Johnson and John H. Leith, *A Reformed Reader: A Sourcebook in Christian Theology*, vol. 1, *Classical Beginnings 1519–1799* (Louisville, Kentucky, Westminster John Knox Press, 1993)

Elaine Kaye, *Mansfield College, Oxford: Its Origin, History and Significance* (Oxford, Oxford University Press, 1999)

N. H. Keeble, *Richard Baxter: Puritan Man of Letters* (Oxford, Oxford University Press, 1982)

Richard Kidd and Graham Sparkes, *God and the Art of Seeing: Visual Resources for a Journey of Faith* (Oxford, Regent's Park College, 2003)

Robert M. Kingdon, 'The Geneva Consistory in the Time of Calvin' in Andrew Pettegree, Alistair Duke and Gillian Lewis (eds.), *Calvinism in Europe 1540–1620* (Cambridge, Cambridge University Press, 1994), pp. 21–34

Beldon Lane, 'The Whole World Singing: A Journey to Iona and Taizé', *Christian Century* (22 March 2000)

Mark Lienhard, 'Luther and the Beginnings of the Reformation' in J.

Raitt, B. McGinn and J. Meyerdorff, *Christian Spirituality: High Middle Ages and Reformation* (London, SCM Press, 1989), pp. 268–99

John Leith, *An Introduction to the Reformed Tradition* (Atlanta, John Knox Press, 1977)

Dairmaid MacCulloch, *Reformation: Europe's House Divided 1490–1700* (London, Penguin, 2003)

George MacLeod, *The Whole Earth Shall Cry Glory* (Glasgow, Wild Goose Publications, 1985)

Hugh MacLeod, 'The Power of the Pulpit' in Clyde Binfield (ed.), *The Cross and the City: Essays in Commemoration of Robert William Dale 1829–1895*, Supplement to the *Journal of the United Reformed Church History Society*, vol. 6 (Supplement no. 2, Spring 1999), pp. 44–55

D. MacMillan, *The Life of George Matheson DD LLD FRSE* (London, Hodder and Stoughton, 1908)

B. L. Manning, 'Effectual Preaching: The Reflexion of One Hearer' in B. L. Manning, *A Layman in the Ministry* (London, The Independent Press, 1942), pp. 135–51

Murdo Ewan Mcdonald, 'D. M. Baillie – as a Student Saw Him' in David Fergusson (ed.), *Christ, Church and Society: Essays on John Baillie and Donald Baillie* (Edinburgh, T. & T. Clark, 1993), pp. 281–7

Elsie Anne McKie (ed.), *John Calvin: Writings on Pastoral Piety* (Mahwah NJ, Paulist Press, 2001)

J. T. McNeil, *The History and Character of Calvinism* (Oxford, Oxford University Press, 1954)

John McTavish, 'John Updike and the Funny Theologian', *Theology Today*, vol. 48, no. 4 (Jan. 1992), pp. 413–25

Robert L. Mentzer, 'The Reformed Churches of France and the Visual Arts' in Paul C. Finney (ed.), *Seeing Beyond the Word: Visual Arts and the Calvinist Tradition* (Grand Rapids, Eerdmans, 1999), pp. 199–230

Ann Murray, 'The Religious Background of Vincent van Gogh and Its Relation to His Views on Nature and Art', *Journal of the American Academy of Religion*, vol. 66 (1978) (1), p. 66

Gordon Mursell, *English Spirituality: From Earliest Times to 1700* (London, SPCK, 2001)

Mark Noll, *America's God: From Jonathan Edwards to Abraham Lincoln* (Oxford, Oxford University Press, 2002)

Henri Nouwen, *The Return of the Prodigal: A Story of Homecoming* (London, Darton, Longman and Todd, 1994)

Geoffrey F. Nuttall, *The Holy Spirit in Puritan Faith and Experience* (Oxford, Blackwells, 1947)

G. F. Nuttall, *Visible Saints: The Congregational Way 1640–1660* (Oxford, Basil Blackwell, 1957)

G. F. Nuttall, 'The First Nonconformists' in G. F. Nuttall and Owen Chadwick (eds.), *From Uniformity to Union 1662–1962* (London, SPCK, 1962), pp. 151–87

Hughes Oliphant Old, *Worship Reformed According to Scripture* (Louisville, Westminster John Knox Press, 2002)

John Oman, *Grace and Personality* (Cambridge, Cambridge University Press, 1925)

David Peel, *Reforming Theology* (London, United Reformed Church, 2002)

J. L. Price, *The Dutch Republic in the Seventeenth Century* (Basingstoke, MacMillan, 1998)

Larry Rasmussen (ed.), *Reinhold Niebuhr: Theologian of Public Life* (London, Collins, 1988)

Howard Rice, *Reformed Spirituality – An Introduction for Believers* (Atlanta, Westminster John Knox Press, 1991)

Gordon Rupp, *Patterns of Reformation* (London, Epworth Press, 1969)

Ziauddin Sardar and Merryl Wyn Davies, *Why Do People Hate America?* (Duxford, Icon Books, 2002)

Simon Schama, *Rembrandt's Eyes* (London, Allen Lane, The Penguin Press, 1999)

Sandra Schneiders, 'Christian Spirituality: Definition, Methods and Types' in Philip Sheldrake (ed.), *The New SCM Dictionary of Christian Spirituality* (London, SCM Press, 2005)

Alan P. F. Sell, *The Great Debate: Calvinism, Arminianism and Salvation* (Worthing, H. E. Walter, 1983)

Norman Shanks, *Iona, God's Energy: The Spirituality and Vision of the Iona Community* (London, Hodder and Stoughton, 1999)

Philip Sheldrake, *Spirituality and History* (London, SPCK, 1991)

Kathryn Spink, *A Universal Heart: The Life and Vision of Brother Roger of Taizé* (London, SPCK, 1986)

George Starr, 'Art and Architecture in the Hungarian Reformed Church' in Paul C. Finney (ed.), *Seeing Beyond the Word: Visual Arts and the Calvinist Tradition* (Grand Rapids, Eerdmans, 1999), pp. 301–40

Harry Stout, *The New England Soul: Preaching and Religious Culture in Colonial New England* (Oxford, Oxford University Press, 1986)

George Stroup, *Reformed Reader: A Sourcebook in Christian Theology*, vol. 2, *Contemporary Trajectories 1799–present* (Louisville, Kentucky, Westminster John Knox Press, 1993)

John H. Taylor, 'Thomas Slade Jones and Vincent van Gogh: a Note', *Journal of the United Reformed Church History Society*, vol. 6 (2002), no. 10, pp. 758–60

David M. Thompson, *Stating the Gospel: Formulations and Declarations of Faith from the Heritage of the United Reformed Church* (Edinburgh, T. & T. Clark, 1990)

Lukas Vischer, 'The Reformed Family World-wide – a Survey' in Jean-Jacques Bauswein and Lukas Vischer (eds.), *The Reformed Family World-wide – a Survey* (Grand Rapids, Eerdmans, 1999)
Lukas Vischer, *Pia Conspiratio: Calvin on the Unity of the Church* (Geneva, John Knox International Reformed Centre, 2000)

Gordon Wakefield, 'Spirituality' in Gordon Wakefield (ed.), *A Dictionary of Christian Spirituality* (London, SCM Press, 1993)
R. S. Wallace, *Calvin's Doctrine of the Word and Sacraments* (Edinburgh, Scottish Academic Press, 1953)
J. R. Watson, *The English Hymn* (Oxford, Oxford University Press, 1997)
Isaac Watts, *A Guide to Prayer* (abridged and edited by Harry Escott: London, Epworth Press, 1948)
David Weir, *The Origins of Federal Theology in Sixteenth Century Reformation Thought* (Oxford, Oxford University Press, 1990)
Anton Wessels, *'A Kind of Bible': Vincent van Gogh as Evangelist* (London, SCM Press, 2000)
Rowan Williams, *The Wound of Knowledge: Christian Spirituality from the New Testament to St John of the Cross* (London, Darton, Longman and Todd, 1979)
Rowan Williams, *Why Study the Past? The Quest for the Historical Church* (London, Darton, Longman and Todd, 2005)
Olive Wyon, *The School of Prayer* (London, SCM Press, 1943)
Olive Wyon, *Living Streams* (London, SCM Press, 1963)

Beverley Zink-Sawyer, 'The Word Purely Preached and Heard: The Listeners and the Hermeneutical Endeavour', *Interpretation*, vol. 51, no. 4 (Oct. 1997), pp. 342–58